Equipped to Counsel

Equipped to Counsel

A collection of thoughts, devotions, and encouragement for helpers

BRITTANY N. ROBERTS

Equipped to Counsel

All Scripture quotations, unless otherwise indicated, are taken from the Holy Bible, New International Version®, NIV®. Copyright ©1973, 1978, 1984, 2011 by Biblica, Inc.™ Used by permission of Zondervan. All rights reserved worldwide. www.zondervan.comThe "NIV" and "New International Version" are trademarks registered in the United States Patent and Trademark Office by Biblica, Inc.™

Soft cover ISBN: 979-8-218387600

For Worldwide Distribution. Printed in U.S.A.

This book is dedicated to all the helpers out there. You are seen, you are heard, you are loved, you are equlpped for this.

INTRODUCTION

One night, I had just gotten out of a pretty difficult counseling session. I was feeling the weight of the conversation, the anxiety, the imposter syndrome, the doubt, and then the discouragement set in. I had gently closed my laptop and just plopped across my bed. I needed a Word from God, some encouragement, something. My emotions were telling me that I needed to go get that vanilla and caramel nutty buddy that I had in the freezer. After debating and almost giving into my craving for sweets, I pulled out my phone to go to the Bible app and look for a devotional.

As I searched, I couldn't find something specifically for what I felt I needed. I went to Instagram and browsed one of the many pages I follow for Christian counselors and nothing. At this point, I was like okay, I know if I go to Amazon I will find exactly what I need. I took to Amazon and typed in "equipped to counsel." Those were the exact words that came to mind. However, I still didn't find what I needed. I searched and searched and searched but couldn't find exactly what I was looking for: some type of devotional specifically for counselors. And I'm not saying they don't exist because I am sure they are out there somewhere, but my searches didn't yield any results. I ended up just exiting off and putting my phone down. I laid there, said a prayer, and went to sleep.

I was discouraged after that session. I needed to be reminded that God had equipped me to do this. I needed to be reminded that I am capable. I needed to be reminded not to give up on myself. I needed to be encouraged. I was looking for a Word, a story, an example, something to lift me up when I was feeling so down and questioning my ability to actually help people.

The next morning, I still had that feeling. I began to just wish there was some kind of devotion specifically for counselors out there. As I went about my day, "equipped to counsel" was on my mind again. It was then that I felt this question in my spirit, "why don't you create what you are looking for?" And I guess you can put together the pieces of the rest because here we are with Equipped to Counsel. *Praise the Lord!*

I don't know if you find yourself like me some days, but I would imagine that you may have had an interaction or two with a client before that left you questioning yourself. I can imagine that you may have felt that anxiety, doubt, frustration, and discouragement too. *(If you haven't, well, please let a sister in on your secret!)*

Regardless of where you find yourself, my sincere hope for this book is that the thoughts, reflections, and devotions on these next pages encourage you. I pray that they would speak to your core and remind you of who you are and Whose you are. Whether you choose to read one thought a day or grab this book as needed, I pray that it will provide you the peace, tranquility, hope, empowerment or whatever else you may stand in need of as you counsel those in your care. I pray that you would let the Word of God wash over you and transform your life and how you counsel.

| 1 |
"For such a time as this"

*"For if you remain silent at this time, relief and deliverance for the Jews will arise from another place, but you and your father's family will perish. And who knows but that you have come to your royal position **for such a time as this**?" - Esther. 4:14*

In the book of Esther, we learn about a king named Xerxes who was searching for a new queen. Eventually a Jewish woman named Esther found favor with him and was chosen to be his new queen. While in the palace, Esther learned of a decree that the Jews (her people) were to be assassinated. But it was custom that the queen could only speak to the king at designated times, so she had two choices: remain silent and let her people perish or risk death and approach the king.

Through her uncle Mordecai, Esther was reminded of her unique position (Esther 4:14) and proximity to the king, the very person who could change the edict to kill the Jews. While God certainly could have used another person, he placed Esther in the palace at that point in time. Esther eventually approached the king and the outcome was deliverance to her people (Esther 8:1 - 9:19). God's people.

We may not be in times like Esther, but we are all in a unique position to care for, help, and transform the lives of those in our care. We are not in this field because it's something we randomly decided to do. We were called and equipped for this work. You were called and equipped for this work fellow helper.

With the knowledge that you have and the things that you have overcome. The education you have. The things you feel that you may lack. With all the skills and qualities that you feel you don't have, you were created for such a time as this.

<u>Read:</u>

Ephesians 2:10 ESV

<u>Reflect:</u>

What qualities, experiences, and/or gifts has God equipped me with to carry out this work of counseling?

| 2 |

Lean in

Sometimes our problems stare us straight in the face in the form of a client.

I remember sitting in an initial assessment one day and having the thought, "thanks for sending me me God." I was taken aback. Here comes this new client experiencing the very thing that I was struggling with myself. This thing that I often tried to conceal and avoid.

I could have easily come up with an excuse for why I couldn't see the client – I didn't have the availability, I was booked. None of those things would have been true but they would have been an easy way to escape problems I didn't wish to face.

I believe that God uses our time with certain clients to highlight the very things we need to address. It's almost as if He is putting a mirror to our face. In these instances, our job is not to have all the answers, but to sit with our clients in their circumstances. To lean in with curiosity, just as with any other client.

I've seen two things happen: 1) my client walk away with clarity and 2) I walk away encouraged. The session not only benefited my client but it also helped me clarify things in my own life.

Psalm 32:8 says, "I will instruct you and teach you in the way you should go; I will counsel you with my loving eye on you."

Sometimes, God might do this by putting a mirror to your face in the form of a client. Just remember to lean in fellow helper.

Reflect:

Are there concerns in my life that I have been actively avoiding? Are there clients I am working with that God might want me to learn from? To lean in to?

Truth for today:

Even if I have concerns I am personally wrestling with, I am still equipped for this.

| 3 |

Out of my Depths

Hey fellow helper, have you ever longed so deeply to help a client? Like the pain that you can clearly see them facing sometimes leaves you feeling helpless? Like you are out of your depths? If you are in this profession, I'd imagine that you may have experienced this at least once or twice.

A client presents with a pain so deep, so unbearable, that no intervention, nod, empathetic remark, validation, or encouragement seems like it will do?

The hurt of desperately wanting to help your client but knowing that you feel inadequate to do so is a difficult feeling to wrestle with. So what do you do?

Well, first, its a good practice to pause and take a deep breath. To let out the weight of responsibility that we are holding on to. Then we give it back to God.

I immediately think of Job, one of God's faithful servants. Job was not foreign to pain and suffering. Job would be that client that would make me feel out of my depths. He lost his children, all his possessions, and his good health. How in the world might I help him?

Read: Job 1 & 2

As a helper, we can place an enormous amount of pressure on ourselves to be the answer, to provide the healing, to say the right things. But we must remember that we are not God nor our client's savior. While God can and will use us to aid in our client's time of need, we must be careful of taking on the responsibility to be THE answer.

You may encounter a client with a deep rooted trauma, a terminal diagnosis, grief, and so many other challenges. Many times it's our willingness to sit with our client that makes the greatest impact.

If we look back to Job's story, his friends sat with him for seven days and seven nights without saying a word (Job 2: 13). Jobs friends comforted him. However, the moment they began to speak Job became upset calling them "miserable comforters" (Job 16:1-5). Their words consisted of unwanted advice, questions, and criticisms.

When you feel out of your depths remember that your presence goes a lot farther than your words may go.

Prayer:

God, I just want to thank you for [Insert client name]. Thank you that I get the opportunity to meet with him/her in their time of need. You know [Insert client name] completely. You know his/her thoughts. You know his/her pain. You know what is said and unsaid. I feel out of my depths to help him/her but God I know that nothing is out of your reach. I just ask that you would guide me and show me the best approach as I meet with them. In our time together, would you begin to provide the healing, comfort, and words that [Insert client name] needs. Have your way Lord. Amen.

Truth for today:

When I feel out of my depths, God will guide me and give tools.

| 4 |

Way Maker

The song Way Maker by Nigerian gospel singer, Sinach, is a beautiful song about how God can make a way when it feels like there is no way. As I reflect on the lyrics of this song, two lines jump out about God working and moving even if we don't see it.

A lot of times I think we forget this truth. We convince ourselves that God isn't working or we question "where are you God?" I know I've done it plenty of times in my life. I've questioned God's presence and his ability to change a situation. I've questioned God's plan for my life and sometimes for my client's life too.

What I realized is that our human tendency is to try to make sense of things. We stop at nothing to have that understanding. But these two lines of this song remind us that just because we don't have the evidence, the understanding, or the ability to see and feel God moving, does not mean that He isn't. God is always moving. He is always working. Always.

Consider the testimony of Joseph, one of 12, whose brothers sold him into slavery. I imagine he thought his life was over. That he was doomed. Yet God was moving ahead of him and lives were changed.

Read: Genesis 37 & 45

The truth is that God's plans may not always look how we imagined. We may not understand various circumstances or situations. We may not always see Him or feel Him moving. His timing may not perfectly align with ours but he is always moving. He makes a way even when there seems to be no way.

Let's stand with expectant hope that he is working in our life and in our client's lives fellow helper.

Prayer:

God you are perfect. You have a purpose and a plan far greater than I can see, think, or imagine. Sometimes I don't feel you or see you, but God I want to trust that you are moving. I want to believe that you will make a way. You create paths that man could never design. Would you help me to believe that you are moving? Would you help my clients to believe as well? They may or may not know you at this moment Lord, but I pray that they would begin to believe that their situation can improve. That change can happen. Lord, use me to instill hope. Not only this, but remind me of Who you are and what only you can do. You are the way maker and the miracle worker. Help me to trust in you today. Amen.

| 5 |

Let Go

There is a picture that I use to see floating around social media. It was an image of a young girl crying because another figure, representing God, wanted her to give Him the teddy bear she was holding. She is pictured crying as she states, "but I love it." What the young girl didn't see was that God had something better, a larger teddy bear, behind his back that He wanted her to have.

I imagine that I may be very similar to the young girl in this image, holding tight to a thing, a dream, a wish, an outcome, whereas God is pleading that I give it to Him.

You bet that it's happened with a client. Imagine this: A client comes in for a crisis. Their world is seemingly falling apart and they have no idea what to do or how to pick up the pieces. You as the clinician long so desperately to help the client. For them to know that it's going to be okay. That things can get better. They leave and you still feel weighed down, wondering, hoping that their time with you helped them feel even a slight bit of relief.

In this work we may have clients that pull on our heart strings a little more than others. Maybe for you it's the client who can't see past the pain, the break-up, the divorce, the miscarriage, the grief. What I have come to learn is that just like the little girl holding the teddy bear, I have to let go of my clients.

Letting go does not mean that I don't care. It simply means that I surrender the outcome to God. It means I trust that the God who sees their sorrow and collects their tears will redeem and restore what is lost or broken in my client's life.

The same goes for you fellow helper. Maybe it's not a client but you recognize that you have been holding onto something that you need to let go.

Stand still knowing that God sees you too. He sees your tears and knows what you stand in need of. As you let go of _ _ _ _, trust that He can and will restore and supply your every need. Trust that what He has in store is "better." So let go today fellow helper.

Read:

Ephesians 3:20-21 NIV

Song for further encouragement:

"Let Go" by DeWayne Woods

| 6 |

Connected to The Vine

"I am the vine; you are the branches. If you remain in me and I in you, you will bear much fruit; apart from me you can do nothing." - John 15:5 NIV

This verse is one that has stuck with me as I entered this profession. I can do no thing without God. It is one that we all would benefit from holding on to.

If you think about the physiology of a vine and branch, a branch alone is not very useful for much. Sure, it may serve as a great tool to fend off dogs or other predators if you are on a walk. It could also be a nice resource to get a camp fire going. However, alone, a branch cannot produce much of anything. It is only when it is connected to a vine that life and resources can be produced.

It is only when we are connected to the True Vine - God, that we can produce anything. A part from Him, our efforts fall short and we cannot produce anything.

As a clinician, we must be mindful of times we are trying to operate outside of our design. Meaning that we need to make sure we are connected to the vine. I vividly remember the day that God convicted me about this. *Why try to do this without me?* I felt Him asking. It was then that I was reminded of why I needed to remain connected to Him. Why I wanted to be connected. God knows our clients fellow helper. He knows how He designed them, their quirks, their fears, their deepest pain. No matter how long we spend assessing a client, He is all-knowing.

Trying to counsel a client without God is like trying to put something together without the instruction manual. You'd likely struggle to put it together.

Fellow helper, as you are connected to Him, He will steer and guide you. Invite Him to help you work with your clients today.

Prayer:

God, I just thank you that you are an ever-present help in my time of need. Your Word reminds me so in Psalm 46:1. I need you today Lord. As I sit with my clients, I recognize that I can do nothing apart from you. Would you lead me, guide me, and strengthen me today? I don't want to do this work without you. Amen.

Reflect:

How might inviting God to help you transform your work with clients?

| 7 |

Let God be God

Have you ever heard the phrase, "Let God be God?" Maybe you've seen it circling social media? What comes to mind when you hear it?

For me, this phrase is a gentle reminder to take my hands off of a situation. Maybe it's something I am trying to control or make happen on my own strength, I need to step aside and give God control. This is especially true when it pertains to clients.

I'll be the first to admit that occasionally when a client leaves, I think of something I wish I said. I wonder if they found the session helpful or beneficial. I wonder if I should have or could have done more for them. I carry these things with me. Wondering, curious, concerned about them until the next session comes.

How about you? Maybe you experienced this recently. Maybe a specific client comes to mind.

Matthew 11:28-29 states, *"Come to Me, all you who are weary and burdened, and I will give you rest. Take My yoke upon you and learn from Me; for I am gentle and humble in heart, and you will find rest for your souls. For My yoke is easy and My burden is light."*

This scripture reminds us to carry our burdens to Jesus. When we do this, we are letting God be God.

Whether you are carrying your client's burdens or your own, they are too heavy for you to carry on your own fellow helper. Take them to God today, to experience rest. Release them and let God be God so that you may receive the relief that He longs to give you.

Reflect:

Whose burdens are you carrying? What do you need release to God?

Prayer:

Lord I have been carrying burdens that you never intended me to carry. As a result I have felt weary, overwhelmed, and restless. Lord I release _______ to you today. I choose to let you be God and I am stepping aside. I am surrendering. My hands are off. I let go Father. I bring it all, every worry, to you today so that your peace may dwell in me. Thank you for carrying my burdens. Thank you for rest. Thank you for relief. Thank you Jesus. Amen.

| 8 |

Capacity

If there was one thing you wish people in your life understood about your role as a therapist what might you say? What is it that you'd want those in your life to know?

For me, I would want them to understand that some days my capacity is limited and while I love them, sometimes I just need to have some quiet time. Sometimes it's hard to talk after work. Some days I just want to lay on the couch and watch tv. Some days I don't want to answer calls or facetimes after work. Some days I'd prefer a relaxing night in the house. Some days.

As I was talking with my coworker about this, we both agreed that there are times that we leave work and just don't want to do anything. Our capacity to fully be present for other things is just low.

If we are honest, we can all reach this point at times. The work we do can be tiring. This isn't a complaint, it's just a truth that comes with working in this field. So naturally, we might need time for ourselves. Time to rest.

In Genesis 2:2-3 we see that God finished the work that he had done, and he rested on the seventh day. Later in the Bible, we are introduced to the word 'sabbath' which means a day of rest. God constantly speaks to the Israelites in the Old Testament about having a Sabbath day of complete rest. It was actually a punishable offense to ignore the Sabbath (Numbers 15:35). And while we are not in times like the

Israelites, I wonder how we might benefit from a Sabbath day in modern times?

Maybe for you this is Sundays when you attend church and rest? Maybe you set aside a specific day during the week where you don't see clients? Maybe it looks another way? The point of a Sabbath was to cease doing any work with the intention of honoring and worshiping God.

When we spend time with God, devoting time for rest and worship, we honor God and experience a renewed capacity and a refreshing. Don't you long for that fellow helper? I know I do!

Reflect:

What ways have you incorporated Sabbath rest into your schedule? What ways could you incorporate this rest moving forward?

Truth for today:

Taking time to rest and cease from working is necessary.

| 9 |

My Strength

Hey fellow helper! Have you ever found it hard to pick yourself up some days? Like you wake up, get dressed, but you're having a slow start to the morning? Maybe the coffee or tea isn't really cutting it? You just feel a bit sluggish and "off"? A little fatigued?

I believe this constant fatigue is why many leave the profession. Years of helping can lead to compassion fatigue and burn out. Helping others, though rewarding, can also be tiring.

This is why it is important to practice self-care and implement rest, but I'd also like to remind us of another tool: tapping into our source of strength.

In 2 Corinthians 12:9-10, God tells Paul, *"My grace is sufficient for you, for my power is made perfect in weakness." Paul responds, "Therefore I will boast all the more gladly about my weaknesses, so that Christ's power may rest on me. That is why, for Christ's sake, I delight in weaknesses, in insults, in hardships, in persecutions, in difficulties. For when I am weak, then I am strong."*

God reminds us that we can look to Him in times of weakness. Our creator, our redeemer, our hope, our strength. Paul experienced weakness in the form of a thorn that was given to him, but in this weakness he learned the sufficiency of God's grace. God reminded Paul that His grace sustains and strengthens. This same grace is available to us.

Sometimes we need rest and time for self-care, but we may also need to fall on our knees an cry out to Him in our weakness. Sometimes its spending time in His presence and seeking Him. Sometimes it is rehearsing Truth and speaking it over yourself throughout the day. As we turn to Him, He will strengthen you, your family, your friends, even your clients.

Many days when I am feeling depleted, I may close my office door and turn on worship music and pray before my first client arrives. As I gear up for my day and feel that I need a little more strength to get me going, I remember to look to God. For when I am weak, He is strong.

Our God is available and just waiting for you to tag him in fellow helper. He's waiting for you to call out to Him. Know that His grace is sufficient and His strength can carry you through your day.

Prayer:

Lord please strengthen me today. I feel sluggish, tired, and as if I have nothing left to give. Your Word tells me that when I am weak, you are strong. I ask that you would strengthen me as I counsel those in my care today. Allow me to rely on your strength and not my own. I need you Father. It's in your name I pray. Amen.

Read:

Psalm 73:26 NIV

| 10 |

"Eloquent words"

Have you ever had a thought that sounds great in your head but the moment you open your mouth it sounds like gibberish?

Sometimes we have things to say but it just doesn't come out how we planned it. Sometimes we think we are sharing something encouraging but it sounds more like a judgment. Sometimes our words may just fail us and we have nothing to say at all. Sometimes we doubt our ability to speak about certain things.

These things have happened to me on numerous occasions in a session. I have something to highlight to a client in session, yet it comes out in a way that I didn't intend or I get tripped up on my own words. Early on in the profession, it would cause discouragement. I was so focused on saying the "wrong thing" that I would just stick to my 'mhmmms' and head nods. Nowadays, I take my time or I might just laugh it off with my client.

Some of you might resonate with the former example. You may find it discouraging when something doesn't come out as planned and resort to more silence in session. It is in these moments that we can ask God to teach us and help us speak to our clients.

Read: Exodus 4:1-12

In this passage Moses was having a very interesting conversation with God. It was a conversation where he was sharing his doubts about the ability to speak to the Israelites.

"I have never been eloquent," Moses shares (v. 10). But God's response to Moses was, "Who gave human beings their mouths? Who makes them deaf or mute? Who gives them sight or makes them blind? Is it not I, the Lord? Now go; I will help you speak and will teach you what to say." (vs. 11-12). Though Moses didn't bite and still asked God to use someone else, I am encouraged by Gods response to Moses: "I will help you speak and teach you what to say."

Whether we question our ability to speak "eloquently," are discouraged, don't know how to respond to a client, falter with our words, or experience some other struggle, we can trust that God can also help us speak and teach us what to say or ask our clients.

I have personally seen Him work in countless sessions and He will do the same for you fellow helper. We don't always have to live in fear of what to say.

Prayer:

God, thank you. Thank you that when my words fail, you are with me and will teach me what I should say. Thank you that you hear me. Lord, I pray against any doubt, hesitation, or discouragement that may arise when I speak to clients. You have entrusted me to do this work and I ask that you would allow me to speak to those in my care with grace, love, boldness, and truth. Lord please use me, guide me, and continue to help me with my words. It is in your name that I pray. Amen.

Prayer

Lord thank you for the compassion and empathy that you have placed within me. Thank you for the ability to sit with my clients and empathize with them. To encourage them. Today I lift up my clients who are desperate to be better. The clients who are longing for a change in their condition or circumstances.

Lord, I thank you for the opportunity to meet with them in their desperation. Lord I know that only you can truly meet the needs of my clients. I know that you are the source from which strength, hope, healing, and peace come from. Help my clients to experience that today. Lord would you wrap your arms around them and allow them to experience your comfort. Would you water the seed of hope that they are holding on to? Lord, guide me and speak through me so that my clients may begin to find the clarity and the direction that they may be longing for.

It's in your name I pray.

Amen.

| 11 |

A letter to you

Hey fellow helper,

You are not inadequate for struggling with your own mental health. You are a human being with real feelings, emotions, thoughts, and experiences. Though difficult to swallow, its a beautiful, humbling reminder that we are not superhuman. We cannot do it all.

Consider the time that Jesus took to step away and care for himself in the Garden of Gethsemane? He was deeply bothered and needed a moment alone to go pray.

Read: Matthew 26:36

There are days when I feel distant, anxious, or sad. It makes it hard to show up for work. It makes me feel like an imposter at times.

"How can I sit across from [client] and help him when I can't even seem to get myself together," I wonder.

What I have learned is that many times my personal struggles help me better empathize and work with my clients. On the other hand, it also reminds me of my humanness. It reminds me that sometimes I need to step back. Our first duty is: do no harm. In order to do so, there may be days that we need to take a day or take multiple days in order to care for ourselves. And there is absolutely nothing wrong with that.

Regardless of where you find yourself, if you are struggling with your own mental health, it doesn't make you less than. It doesn't mean you are a "bad" therapist. It doesn't disqualify you from being able to do your job. But let it remind you that you too are a human in need of intentional time and care just like the clients you sit across from daily.

With love,

A fellow human

| 12 |

Community

God's original design was for us to be in community. He created us to operate as a people. A body. We see this from the beginning of time and creation.

"The Lord God said, "It is not good for the man to be alone. I will make a helper suitable for him." - Genesis 2:18

I believe that community can be a difficult topic for many because we all have experienced some sort of hurt by people. We may have even caused hurt in our lifetime. However, a common theme shown throughout the Bible is that we need people.

One of my favorite passages that demonstrates this truth can be found in Exodus 17. The Israelites had just crossed the Red Sea and watched their enemies get swallowed up by the waters (Exodus 14) but shortly after, they were under attack. Moses told Joshua to gather some men and go fight while he would go stand on the top of the hill with the staff of God in his hands (vs.9). So Joshua did as Moses said, while Moses, Aaron, and Hur made their way to the top of the hill. The text states that as long as Moses held up his hands, the Israelites were winning, but whenever he lowered his hands, the Amalekites were winning (vs.11). Eventually Moses grew tired, so Aaron and Hur played a crucial role in helping Moses keep his hands up so the Israelites could win the battle (vs. 12).

In our field of counseling, we too need Aaron's and Hur's. We need men and women we can consult with and seek out for support with challenging clients, learn from, and possibly receive guidance.

It may be challenging to seek out others especially if you do not work in a team setting, however having good relationships with other clinicians or a strong support system is beneficial for many reasons. Especially in our line of work.

<u>Reflect:</u>

Is having a good support system/being in community important to you? Why or why not?

Do you have a support network or clinician(s) you can consult with?

Who are they?

| 13 |

In His Image

When I started my first full-time counseling position, I would shrink back and approach sessions in a timid way. This looked like:

- Holding back thoughts or questions
- Shying away from personal disclosure that may be helpful
- Tiptoeing around certain conversations
- Trying to conceal my responses or emotions
- Too much silence

Part of this was my own insecurity and part was fear but what I now recognize is that showing up as my full authentic self is more beneficial for myself and my clients.

Genesis 1:27 says, "God created mankind in His own image, in the image of God He created them. Male and female, He created them."

That means you. That means me.

Whether it's your empathy, your genuineness, your curiosity, your humor, your creativity, your joy, or your personal challenges and experiences...remember that you were created in the image of God. He gave you those qualities and experiences for a reason and needs you to operate as such. The unique qualities you bring, the thoughts and ideas you have...your client may need.

When you allow the version of yourself crafted and intimately designed by God to show up in your work it's powerful. Not only this, but it benefits you, it benefits your clients, and it pleases God.

Contrary to what you may have been taught, there is no "perfect therapist/school counselor/social worker/etc. mold" that you must fit into. You are made in His image fellow helper. A beautiful image. Show up today and every day as you are.

<u>Reflect</u>:

What traits do you value about yourself and bring into sessions? (i.e my warmth)

Are there things that you feel like you can't show in sessions?

| 14 |

Waves

Some dreams can be scary. Not the dreams where you hope for something to happen in your life. I'm talking about the dreams we experience when we fall into deep sleep. The type of dreams that sometimes wake you up feeling confused, worried, or upset.

I recall a specific dream I had one night where I was at this beautiful beach. I was admiring all of the boats in the water then all of a sudden these huge waves came. I was too close to the shore and had little time to run before the waves came over me. I felt like I was drowning. Every possession I had was wiped away by the water, including myself. Once the waves settled, myself and countless others began to search for our things. With their help, I was able to locate everything that the waves had wiped away.

I felt confused when I woke up but I now know that it was God's encouragement to me. This dream is very much how life can feel. One day we may be enjoying life then suddenly the waves come crashing without warning. These waves take you off course. They interrupt your life. They throw you into a state of confusion, worry, etc.

John 16:33 states, "I have told you these things, so that in me you may have peace. In this world you will have trouble. But take heart! I have overcome the world."

As helpers, we are not exempt from life's challenges and difficulties. We too are constantly learning the best way to navigate the waves that come. So today I want to take time to acknowledge you and the work that you do. You constantly show up and hold space for others while also holding your own personal matters. This can feel lonely at times and I just want you to know that when the waves come crashing and interrupt your plans, your world, and your peace, you are not alone. You will never be left to deal with the aftermath alone.

God offers us His peace with His presence. The waves will come, but so does He. The destruction may happen, but He will restore. Hold on to this hope today.

<u>Reflect:</u>

Take time to read Psalm 23. Read it slowly and aloud. Incorporate deep breaths as you digest what the psalmist is saying.

How does this passage of scripture make you feel?

| 15 |

Imposter

We've all heard of imposter syndrome. Probably experienced it a time or two as well. I don't know a person that hasn't. It can look like questioning your ability, your knowledge, and your preparedness. If you find yourself questioning yourself fellow helper, *welcome to the club!*

I would be lying if I said I only experienced imposter syndrome in the early stages of my career. The truth is, the imposter syndrome has weaved it's way into various parts of my journey. Graduate school, internship, the initial months working my first counseling position, a new client with an odd presentation. It appears, goes away, and then comes back again. *Can I really help this client? Do I really know what I'm doing?*

I once saw someone say that imposter syndrome is the silent killer that often keeps people from walking in their calling. It's the thing that keeps us constantly measuring ourselves and our abilities. It can be one of our greatest enemies. But we must overcome this enemy if we are to truly walk in God's calling for our lives.

Read: 2 Corinthians 10:5

When we begin to question ourselves, we can acknowledge it, explore it, and take it captive, rather than allowing it to preoccupy us. We can remind ourselves of God's truth that He equipped us for this work. It is only then that we will be able to operate as the helper He has called us to be.

So the next time imposter syndrome comes fellow helper, tell it that it has to go and let it lead you to a place of reflection and remembrance of who you really are...*a good daggone helper :)*

<u>Reflect:</u>

When you begin to experience imposter syndrome, what have you found to be helpful? Anything unhelpful?

| 16 |

Breath of Life

Would you close your eyes and take a deep breath with me?

Breathe in, 2, 3, 4

Hold, 2, 3, 4

Breathe out, 2, 3, 4

Let's do it again, but this time as you breathe out imagine breathing away the worry, the doubt, the anxiety, the uncertainty, the heaviness, the pressure, the discouragement you may feel.

I want you to breathe it out and leave it there. Blow it as far away as you possibly can.

Read: Ezekiel 37: 1-14

In this passage, we learn that the prophet Ezekiel is standing in a valley of dry bones. When I visualize this, I imagine dessert like conditions and an absence of life. God speaks to Ezekiel in that valley and tells him that He will bring life back to those dry bones.

From this passage we learn that God not only brings life but He also restores it. Where we may feel empty, He can restore. Where we may feel numb, He can bring life. Where we may feel hopeless, He can revive.

Pause and take a few more deep breaths with me fellow helper. As you breathe in, take in God's breath of life. Sometimes I like to do this outside, allowing the fresh air to fill my lungs, experiencing the sensation of air enter my body.

Maybe you are feeling depleted work. Maybe you feel that you have lost your empathy and compassion for others.

Maybe you are feeling pretty numb and mellow. Breathe in His breath of life. Allow this breath to bring you life and restoration.

<u>Prayer:</u>

God I feel dry, mellow, and depleted. I pray that you would bring life back to my bones. I pray that I would experience a renewed passion and joy for this work of counseling. When I breathe in would you allow me to experience a refreshing? And when I breathe out would you allow the weight and heaviness to leave? God, thank you for listening to me. You know what I need before I even ask. Lord I thank you that I get to be in relationship with you. Thank you for the life and restoration I know I will begin to experience again. Amen.

| 17 |

God in me

I heard a Pastor once say that we don't hesitate to believe in the power of God to move mountains but we doubt the power of God in us. Simply put, we don't believe God's ability to use us.

This brings to my mind the disciples in their earlier stages of walking with Jesus.

Read: Matthew 17: 14-21

In this short passage, the disciples ask Jesus, why they couldn't drive the demon out. Jesus responded, "Because you have so little faith. Truly I tell you, if you have faith as small as a mustard seed, you can say to this mountain, 'Move from here to there,' and it will move. Nothing will be impossible for you."

Fast forward to the book of Acts and we learn that Jesus has gone to the Father, the Holy Spirit has come upon the disciples, and those same disciples are now performing **many** miracles.

If there is one thing that I have learned by being in this profession it is that God can and will use me just as He did the disciples and many others. When I exercise faith and believe, He makes the seemingly impossible, possible. It is not my own doing but God working in me, that accomplishes these things.

Philippians 2:13 says, "For God is working in you, giving you the desire and the power to do what pleases him."

God lives inside of us and as we continue to walk with Him and experience proximity to Him, we too will begin to believe in our ability to "move mountains."

Truth for today:

God's power is available to me and can work in and through me to do the impossible.

Prayer:

Father I thank you that you live within me. I thank you that you long to use me and help others come to know you. Lord, I know that I doubt your power and ability to use me at times, but God I come to you and I ask you now: please help me to believe. It's in your name I pray, Amen.

| 18 |

God with me

One of my favorite scriptures is Isaiah 43:2. It states, *"When you pass through the waters, **I will be with you**; and when you pass through the rivers, they will not sweep over you. When you walk through the fire, you will not be burned; the flames will not set you ablaze."*

It's a beautiful reminder that no matter what we face in life, God is with us.

As I read those lines, I think of countless examples in the Bible where this was shown to be true:

- When Moses led the Israelites out of Egyptian captivity in Exodus, God parted the waters of the Red Sea for the Israelites to pass through (Exodus 14). He was with them.

- When Joshua led the Israelites towards the promised land, God parted the rivers of the Jordan for the Israelites to pass through (Joshua 3).

- When King Nebuchadnezzar threw Shadrach, Meshach and Abednego, into a fiery furnace, they were not burned (Daniel 3). God was with them.

Fellow helper, no matter what you face in your life, no matter how difficult things get. No matter how scary the conditions around you may seem, God is with you...always. And this should comfort us.

Let's apply this to working with clients. God is with you in sessions with particularly challenging clients. God is with you when you are lost in a session. God is with you when you feel that you've exhausted all options for helping a client or family. God is with you when your client is experiencing an impossible situation. God is with you in session, between sessions, and out of sessions. He's always with you.

There have been many times in a session that I silently pray to myself, *God I know you are with me, please help me,* and there is absolutely nothing wrong with doing this. In fact, I encourage you to pray the same fellow helper.

Additional Scriptures to read:

Deuteronomy 31:6 & 8

Hebrews 13:5

Joshua 1:5 & 9

Isaiah 41:10

| 19 |

God for me

*"When hard pressed, I cried to the Lord; He brought me into a spacious place. The Lord is with me; I will not be afraid. What can mere mortals do to me? The Lord is with me; **he is my helper**. I look in triumph on my enemies."*
- Psalm 118: 5-7 NIV

Hey fellow helper, did you know that God is for you? Did you know that He fights for you? Cares for you? Hears you? Loves you? Helps you?

God is for YOU. In your weakness, He is for you. In your doubt, He is for you. In your despair, He is for you. In your pain, He is for you. In your mistakes, He is for you.

"God for us" means that He is on our side. He is forever rooting for us and working things out for our good. It means that nothing we do can ever separate us from the love of God.

Romans 8:31 says, "Can anything ever separate us from Christ's love? Does it mean he no longer loves us if we have trouble or calamity, or are persecuted, or hungry, or destitute, or in danger, or threatened with death?"

Continue on to verse 38-39 of Romans 8 and it says, *"And I am convinced that nothing can ever separate us from God's love. Neither death nor life, neither angels nor demons, neither our fears for today nor our worries about tomorrow— not even the powers of hell can separate us from God's love. No power in the sky above or in the earth below—indeed, nothing in all creation will ever be able to separate us from the love of God that is revealed in Christ Jesus our Lord."*

Sometimes we experience things in life that may not feel good and make us believe that God isn't for us. Things happen that might make us question His love for us. But in these moments we can rest knowing that God's Word is permanent, unchanging, and true. He is for us today, tomorrow, and always.

Prayer:

God, if I am honest, it's hard to believe that you are for me. It's hard to believe that you love me when my circumstances continue to torment and overwhelm me. Lord would you help me to see the ways that you are for me. Help me to experience your love in a real and tangible way.

Additional Scriptures to read:

Psalm 94: 14

Psalm 18:2-3

Psalm 27:1-3

| 20 |

God for my clients

"See what great love the Father has lavished on us, that we should be called children of God! And that is what we are!"
- 1 John 3:1a

Have you ever sat with a client that presses on your heart strings and you long so desperately to help? A client that is stuck in an abusive situation? A hopeless client? An anxious client? A client with a long history of trauma? Did you know that just as God is for you, God is for them too?

I can recall numerous times where I have ended a session and I couldn't help but wish my client could experience the love and hope that comes from God. I wished they could experience the peace that can be found in Jesus. I wished I could say more or do more.

Eventually, God reminded me that I don't have to "wish" for it to happen, I could pray that they would come to know and experience the goodness of God. Because the truth is, God wants that more than we do for our clients. **He loves and cares for His children much more than we could ever care for them.**

Hold on to this truth as you sit with your clients today.

Prayer:

God I just pray right now for every client I meet with. Whether they know you or not, I pray that you might use me to show them your love, grace, and compassion. Birth a curiosity within them to know you Lord. God, I know that you are for them so I believe that you will do what only you can do in their life. You will make yourself known to them. Thank you that you love, see, and care for your children. Have your way in their lives. Amen.

Prayer

"Some days it's hard to go to work. Some days it feels like I just need a break. Time to sit with myself. I love the work I do but it can take a toll on me at times. Having to be emotionally present, compassionate, and empathetic can be exhausting. I feel weak but I know that it is only with God that I will be strong. I can only continue this work by being completely dependent and reliant on the Lord. Apart from Him I know that I can't do it." – A fellow helper

---

Lord I thank you that when we are weak, you are strong. 2 Corinthians 12:9 says, that your power is made perfect in our weakness. Lord I feel weak. I need a reset. I need rest. I am so thankful that you have called me to this work but there are times that I start to experience compassion fatigue. Some days I leave work and I feel that I have nothing left to give.

Lord I just ask that you would help me. Would you provide daily space, time, and opportunities for rest? Would you allow me to experience a refreshing? Would you allow me to experience a renewed love and passion for this work? Would you meet me in my weakness?

Lord I acknowledge that I can do nothing apart from you. So today I seek you with my whole heart. I know that you hear my cries, you know my every need, and every need you will supply.

Today I say thank you. I thank you in advance for what you
have already begun to do.
I love you Father, Amen.

| 21 |
Proximity

In my quiet time one morning, I began reading through the New Testament and specifically the book of Matthew. The book opens up by sharing the events leading up to and surrounding the birth of Jesus. If we look to Matthew 1 and 2, there are 3 mentions of an angel of the Lord coming to Joseph and speaking to him. In each conversation or dream, Joseph receives some sort of direction or instruction of where to go next or where to avoid to ensure the safety and protection of his family.

As I reflected on this further, I recognized that Joseph had to stay in close proximity to God and remain open to God's instruction. With God's direction and instruction, Joseph, Mary, and Jesus, remained safe and protected. Apart from it, they may have been lost and in danger.

What I was reminded is that as clinicians, we must also keep close proximity to God and remain open to His instruction. When we sit with our clients we have a unique opportunity to be used by God. To allow God to speak through us to our client. But this can only happen when we stay in close proximity to Him.

I believe that the things laid on our heart to share, the ideas that come to mind in a session, the constant desire to speak on something...they can be a direct result of our proximity to God. They can be divine instruction from the Holy Spirit. Because God does speak, sometimes we just have to listen.

Today, I invite you to ask God to show up in your session. Ask God to speak through you and give you guidance on how best to help a client.

Reflect:

What actions could I take or am I already taking to maintain proximity to God? (ex. Daily prayer, reading my Bible, etc.)

| 22 |
Qualified

Have you ever heard the quote, "God doesn't call the qualified, He qualifies the called."

I am not sure who spoke this popular quote, but I see it's validity and truth. If we look at the many people God used in the Bible, they weren't perfect men and women who spoke to his people, who performed miracles, or who spread the gospel. God called men and women who often struggled with some sort of difficulty, sin, or ailment.

I think of Moses, who God spoke, "I am sending you to Pharaoh to bring my people the Israelites out of Egypt" (Exodus 3:10). As we continue reading, Moses argues with God about his qualifications to be used in that way. However, as I reflect upon their interaction, I am reminded that God provided Moses with the necessary tools to accomplish the work He prepared for him. God tells Moses that He will help him (Exodus 4:12), He called Moses' brother Aaron to assist him (vs. 13-16), and He gave him a staff to perform the miracles (vs. 17). God equipped and qualified Moses for the jobs. Likewise, God qualifies us.

In a world that pressures clinicians to "have it all together" I want you to know that you are worthy to do this work even if you struggle with some sort of difficulty, doubt, or struggle. Whether you take medication, have your own therapist, have challenges with your mental health, have a mental health diagnosis, don't know it all, or have a "bad/off" day. You are still worthy and called for this. Moses felt that his slow speech and tongue disqualified him, yet God still used Him (Exodus 4: 10).

Just as the men and women of the Bible were not immune from struggles and difficulties, we are also not immune, and God can still wants to use us.

Today I want to remind you that no matter the struggle, you are not any less worthy to counsel those in your care. God qualifies the called and He wants to use you to change the lives of His children.

Let's be careful not to disqualify ourselves from doing God's work based on a perceived shortcoming or societal standard.

<u>Read:</u>

1 Corinthians 1:27-29

1 Corinthians 2:1-5

| 23 |

Identity

"For we are his workmanship [His own master work, a work of art], created in Christ Jesus for good works, which God prepared beforehand, that we should walk in them." -
Ephesians 2:10

When I first entered this field of mental health counseling, I was so convinced that I had to fit into this mold of what a therapist looked like. I had to sit a certain way in session. I had to start and end my sessions a certain way. I had to follow a plan and work towards specific goals each session. I had to use certain interventions. I had to say the "right" things.

What I quickly learned is that while some of these things may be important, they shouldn't keep me from counseling as my authentic self. That would be a disservice to God, to myself, and to my clients.

Something I wish I realized earlier on in graduate school is that there is no "one size fits all" type of therapist. There is no "right" way to do therapy. Sure, there are certain ethical guidelines we must follow but when it comes to caring for our clients, there is no absolute approach we <u>must</u> follow.

So what I want you to know today is this:

You are important.
Who you are, all your kinks and quirks are unique.

Your laugh, your thought process, your empathy and compassion is necessary.

Your experiences, your upbringing, your education, your story matters.

Your identity is in Christ.

You are His masterpiece. Specifically designed for a great purpose.

Do not conform. Do not shrink. Do not mold yourself into anything other than who you know yourself to be and who He has created you to be.

Everything that you have endured, every quality you possess, every story you tell has immense value. It makes you the unique therapist that you are today.

You are no Carl Rogers, Irvin Yalom, or Marsha Linehan. God has made you in His image and that's the image that your client's need to see.

Being our full authentic self and showing up in each session as such is one of the best interventions that we can use.

You are so loved fellow helper, as you are.

| 24 |

Way Maker Part II

As I was praying one morning, I began to weep at how good God is. He had just recently answered a prayer that my family and I had been praying for awhile and I couldn't help but just cry at His goodness and faithfulness.

God is a way maker. He is God of the seemingly impossible. He is God of miracles. Sometimes it can be challenging to hold onto hope when you've gone days, months, years, decades with no answer to your prayer but I am confident that God's timing, whether we understand it or not, is absolutely perfect. He makes a way in His timing for His purposes and our good.

Consider the woman with the issue of blood in the Bible. Her story can be found in Luke 8:43-48. For 12 years this woman suffered from a condition causing her to bleed. The Bible states, *"but no one could heal her"* (vs. 43). Mark 5:26-27 indicates that she had gone from doctor to doctor and spent everything she had trying to find answers and be healed however, no one could heal her.

This woman eventually comes into contact with Jesus. She touches His robe and was instantly healed - her bleeding stopped (vs. 44). Jesus tells the woman, *"Daughter, your faith has healed you. Go in peace"* (vs. 48).

Her faith coupled with Jesus' power, allowed her to be healed from a sickness that she endured for 12 years.

Let's put ourselves in this women's shoes for a moment. If I were her, I imagine that I would feel discouraged, desperate, and disappointed. I can't honestly say that I would still have hope to be healed after 12 years. I may have grown angry with God wondering why I had to suffer and couldn't experience a miracle. *How about you? How do you think you would feel?*

In our deepest desperation and prayers, God can make a way. Whether it be for a client who is experiencing an immense amount of pain, a sickness you are praying to be healed from, or someone else in your life. Know that God can make a way. That may look like healing, that may look like a platform to help others with the same condition, or some other way. Nonetheless, God always makes a way.

Prayer:

God I thank you that you are a way maker. Isaiah 43:16 says that you make ways through the sea and a path through mighty waters. You make roads in the wilderness and rivers in the dessert (vs. 19). Nothing is impossible for you to accomplish Lord. God I just pray right now for [insert thing or person], you see them, you know their pain, and you love them deeply. God I ask that you would make a way in their life. Whatever that looks like, I know that you can and will move on their behalf. I trust you, I have faith that you can do it, and I surrender the outcome to you. I love you Lord. Have your way. Amen.

| 25 |

I believe

"As Jesus went on from there, two blind men followed Him, screaming loudly, "Have mercy and compassion on us, Son of David (Messiah)!" When He went into the house, the blind men came up to Him, and Jesus said to them, "Do you believe [with a deep, abiding trust] that I am able to do this?" They said to Him, "Yes, Lord." Then He touched their eyes, saying, "According to your faith [your trust and confidence in My power and My ability to heal] it will be done to you."" - Matthew 9:27-29 AMP

Let's take a closer look at this scripture. "Do you believe that I am able to do this?" This is the question Jesus asked the two blind men before healing them. Do you believe?

This question pierced my heart as I read it. It was as if I could hear God asking me the same question. It echoed in my head....do I believe that He is able to do [this].

I imagine this question might hit each of us in a different way. Maybe there is something in your life you are hoping for but deep down you don't believe it may happen for you. Maybe there is a client who has expressed a desire for something but expects the worse to happen. I believe we've all been there ourselves and we also know someone in our lives thats been there.

So let's look at it through a clinical lens: Do you believe that God can use you? Do you believe that God can help your client? Do you believe that God can help you reach more clients in your private practice? Do you believe that God will help you find a job that works for you and your family? Do you believe that God will help you complete your degree?

Today, take some time to reflect on what it is you may be hoping for and ask yourself if you truly believe that God can do it. Ask Him to help you believe.

<u>Additional reading:</u>

Mark 9:23-25

| 26 |

All the Answers

Hey fellow helper,

Have you ever felt pressure to have every single answer? To have experience with every situation, diagnosis, or concern? To know it all?

At times, I think we all experience undue pressure to have all the answers. Whether that pressure is internal, from our clients, their families, or supervisors, other external influences, pressure can come in many forms.

I remember vividly the day a client left my office and my discouragement set in. I could see all over my clients face that she was disappointed. I felt like I had somehow failed her. I had failed to do my job well. I had failed to provide the answers that she was longing so desperately for.

The truth is, we will never have all the answers. We will never memorize the DSM from cover to cover, know the best modality and treatment for every concern, nor be able to answer every question posed to us.

After that session I had to shut my office door, sit down, and breathe. God lovingly reminded me that He was in control. That He alone is Savior. Not me. He has all the answers. Not me.

Proverbs 3:5-6 says, "Trust in the Lord with all your heart and lean not to your own understanding. In all your ways acknowledge Him and He will direct your paths."

This should encourage us. This should remind us that we don't have to have all the answers because our Father does.

When glaring looks of disappointment pierce our hearts, when discouragement sets in, when thoughts of failure arise, we can be still, close our eyes, breathe, and acknowledge that God knows all, sees all, and will accomplish all things according to His plans.

Relinquish the pressure to have every answer, fellow helper.

Further reading:

Psalm 139:1-18

Romans 11:33-36

Isaiah 55: 8-9

| 27 |

"Too Young"

I will never forget the days working at a Christian sports camp in 2017. I had just graduated with my Bachelors degree and decided to become a camp counselor at *Summer's Best Two Weeks Citikidz* for the summer. At this camp, I had a unique opportunity to care for campers between the ages of 8 - 18 each week.

One week while working in cabin G4 (*high school age girls*), I was met with a discouraged girl after our Bible study. She shared that she was "afraid" to talk about God with her peers because she was "too young." She was crippled by fear believing that her words wouldn't matter and no one would listen.

Immediately, God brought to mind two scriptures which I was able to use to encourage this young woman: *1 Timothy 4:12 and Jeremiah 1:6-8.*

1 Timothy 4:12 states, "And don't be intimidated by those who are older than you; simply be the example they need to see by being faithful and true in all that you do. Speak the truth and live a life of purity and authentic love as you remain strong in your faith."

Jeremiah 1:6-8 says, "Then I said, "Ah, Lord God! Behold, I do not know how to speak, for I am [only] a young man." But the Lord said to me, "Do not say, 'I am [only] a young man,' Because everywhere I send you, you shall go, And whatever I command you, you shall speak. Do not be afraid of them [or their hostile faces], for I am with you [always] to protect you and deliver you," says the Lord.

Years later I have found myself needing the same encouragement and scripture I shared with this young woman.

What I have found is that we all struggle or have struggled with something about ourselves at one point or another. Maybe for you it isn't that you are "too young," but you feel that you are "too old." Maybe too generous, too introverted, or too loud. These things can impact how we live, how we counsel, and what we do or do not do.

Our "too [insert thing]" is likely the very thing that God will use to transform us. It is the thing that will require us to lean closer to Him as He uses us to do His work on earth.

Today I pray that our too youngs, too olds, or too louds, will push us closer to God and not away from the very things that He has called us to and equipped us for.

| 28 |

More

Have you ever wanted to do more for your client? Ever feel like your 50-60 minute session wasn't enough?

I've been there. I've had moments where I know that I am at the end of my session time, yet I don't want to end because we were getting somewhere. I fear that waiting a week might backtrack the progress made. (*Just sharing my honest thoughts here.*) I imagine that I am not alone though. I imagine that I am not the only therapist in the world who has experienced this longing for more time, more resources, more support. More for my client.

What I am reminded of this morning is that we have limitations that we must honor. Whether that be sticking to the allotted time, honoring my time and my clients time, or trusting the therapeutic process.

There is always something more we could hope for in our work with clients, however today I am resting in the truth that while I hope for more, our Father in heaven is the God of more. He is able to do more than we could ever ask or imagine. Ephesians 3:20, tells me so. Let's try to rest in that truth for our clients today.

Prayer:

God I thank you that you are the God of more. While I sometimes wish there was more time, more resources, more support, more that I could provide for my client, I know that you are the God of more. Unlike man, you have no limitations or barriers. You have no restrictions that hinder your ability to move mightily. God I pray for more today. I pray that seeds would be planted in the allotted time that I do have with my clients and you would arrange opportunities for those seeds to be watered, however that may look. Your Word tells me that you can do more than I could ever ask, think, or imagine, so I rest in that truth today believing that you will do more. It's in your name. Amen.

| 29 |

My "why"

If one were to ask you why you do the work that you do, how might you respond? What is your "why"?

I remember the exact moment that I realized I wanted to be a therapist. I had studied Kinesiology in undergrad and I sat in my advisors office just weeks away from graduation and cried because I had no idea what I wanted to do. I was questioning if that was even the field I wanted to be in. I had applied for graduate school, I had looked for jobs in the field, and eventually took an entry level position working in college admissions. I loved my job in Admissions and it was actually the thing that led me to become a therapist.

Day after day I sat on the couch with families exploring what they were looking for in a University. And it dawned on me that I loved sitting with people and talking about life, about decisions, about their wants. After 1 year in my job, I decided to pursue a Master's degree in Clinical Mental Health Counseling. I cared for people and longed to help them. I wanted to create a safe space for people to be heard, to be seen, to heal, to restore hope. But more than anything, I felt God's "yes."

Whether you have been in the field for awhile or are just beginning, I guarantee that you have questioned or will question at least once, if you can do this work. We don't just sit and talk to people as some believe, we do more than that. We explore years of trauma, grief, and pain. We listen to painful stories, buried memories, and so much more. Simply put, the work we do can be heavy.

So if you ever find yourself questioning the work you do, remember that you are not alone fellow helper. In these moments, it can be helpful to look back and consider your why. Consider what led you to the field in the first place.

Scripture to hold on to:

"The Spirit of the Lord God is upon me, because the Lord has anointed me to bring good news to the poor; he has sent me to bind up the brokenhearted, to proclaim liberty to the captives, and the opening of the prison to those who are bound;"

- Isaiah 61:1

Reflect:

What is the reason and/or reasons that I pursued this career?

How does Isaiah 61:1 speak to me or resonate with my work?

| 30 |
Safe

One of my favorite characteristics about God is that He is safe. There is a security that comes from Him that the world, people, or possessions cannot provide. However I'd be remiss to say that this view happened overnight. In actuality I use to be afraid of God. Afraid of his judgment. Afraid that He would cast me out if I made a mistake. Afraid that I couldn't come to Him with my vulnerabilities. I couldn't view Him as safe because I was afraid of Him.

But there is difference between fearing God and being afraid of God. When I fear God, I acknowledge His power and authority. When I am afraid of God, I hide from Him. He's scary. He's not safe.

As I devoted time to building my relationship with the Lord, my view of Him began to change. I began to fear God and also experience the safety that came from His presence.

The Bible has numerous references to safety. Specifically, many writers described God as a safe place or reflected on how He kept them safe in times of trouble or when they were in danger.

The writer of Psalm 91:2 says, *"This I declare about the LORD: He alone is my refuge, my place of safety; he is my God, and I trust him."*

As a helper, we have a unique opportunity to be a safe place for our client. When there is a sense of safety, there is increased vulnerability. There is openness, genuineness, there is an opportunity for healing, there can be relief, and so much more.

But what does that look like? Have you ever paused to consider how you create a safe space for your clients? What do you do? What do you say?

Let's look at how God has shown Himself to be safe in scripture.

Read:

Psalm 23: 1-6

Psalm 46:1-11

Psalm 121:1-8

Reflect:

Do I have a healthy fear of God or am I afraid of God?

Can I think of times that God has shown me He is safe?

In what relationships or spaces do I feel safe?

In what ways do I cultivate a safe space for my clients?

Prayer

Jeremiah 17:7-8 says, "But blessed is the one who trusts in the Lord, whose confidence is in Him. They will be like a tree planted by the water that sends out its roots by the stream. It does not fear when heat comes; its leaves are always green. It has no worries in a year of drought and never fails to bear fruit."

God I thank you that when I place my trust in you, I prosper.

Just as a plant needs water to survive, I recognize that I need you.
You are my source. You are my strength. You are Jehovah Nissi…my provider.
With you I don't have to worry.

Lord help me to place my confidence in you today. When I have a daily choice to trust what I see or to trust you, help me to choose you Jesus. Let me trust you with my life, my family, my clients, and with all of my possessions.

Isaiah 40:31 says, "But those who trust in the Lord will find new strength. They will soar high on wings like eagles. They will run and not grow weary. They will walk and not faint."

Thank you for the new strength that you provide. Thank you that I get to soar high on wings like eagles. Thank you that

you allow me to run and not grow weary, to walk and not
faint.
Thank you that with you I prosper.

You are reliable Father. You are good. You are true. Help me
to depend completely on you today.

It's in Your name I pray.
Amen.

| 31 |

Precious

Hey fellow helper, did you know that you are so precious to God?

There was a time in my life that I knew that (*I had the knowledge*) but I didn't believe it because I didn't feel precious. I was so consumed with the thoughts and opinions of others. I ruminated on how others perceived me not recognizing that I had a heavenly Father who saw me as I was and loved me just the same.

Well just as with any deep-rooted belief, this didn't go away overnight. It didn't go away in a month or two. It happened gradually. My prayer was this: *God help me to see myself the way you see me.*

Today I can say that God has answered that prayer. He is still answering it. Some days I sit and I wonder how did I get here? How did I get to a place of believing in myself? Loving myself? Seeing myself as previous and valuable to God?

Prayer. Quiet time with God. Reading His word. Journaling. Affirmations. They helped me get here. And I pray that you would get there too fellow helper. There is such an overwhelming joy that can bring you to tears when you recognize just how precious you are to Him. It will transform your life, your relationships, the way you live, the way you counsel, and operate.

So know this today..."*You are precious to me.*" - *God*

Read:

Psalm 139:1-18 NLT

Prayer:

God I thank you that I get to experience your love. Sometimes it can be hard to believe that I am precious in your sight, but even now, I ask that you would you change my perspective of myself. Help me to see myself the way you see me Father. Help me to experience the freedom and transformation that comes from knowing your love and thoughts for me. Help me to fix my gaze on you, what you say, and what you think about me. Silence the voices, thoughts, and opinions of those around me so that your voice may stand out. I want to know how precious I am to you Lord. It's in your name I pray.

Amen.

| 32 |

Pray

"In the morning, Lord, you hear my voice; in the morning I lay my requests before you and wait expectantly." - Psalm 5:3

One of the joys of this profession is seeing prayers answered in a clients life. Getting to witness the client who was once discouraged, hopeless, and struggling with a difficult situation experience joy, peace, and hope. It truly brings tears to my eyes.

I will never forget the exact moment a client entered my office and week after week I saw a new person. I saw a changed person. Working with her for over a year and seeing the low lows and the in-betweens, she was different. This is what I had hoped for. What I had prayed for. What we worked towards.

Praying for your clients in your quiet time before a session, after a session, or during a session is a powerful thing. Why? Because God hears and He moves.

Sometimes this may look like saying a quick prayer in the moments before session. Maybe it's devoting time after a session or between sessions. Sometimes it may look like praying quietly in your head during the session. There is no wrong way to pray for our clients.

If you are uncertain what to say or how to pray consider this general prayer I may recite prior to a session:

<u>Prayer:</u>

Lord, thank you for [Insert Client Name]. Thank you that you love them and see them. Thank you for allowing me to meet with them. God be with us during this session. Help me to be your vessel. Help me to listen well and be attentive to their needs. It's in your name I pray. Amen.

| 33 |

Peace

"In peace I will lay down and sleep, for you alone Lord, make me dwell in safety." -Psalm 4:8

Do you remember the days where trust falls were a huge thing? Some were pranks, some team building exercises, some to test a person's strength. What I recognize about the trust fall is that no matter the reason for doing it, a trust fall requires one thing...trust. For you to willingly risk the possibility of falling and hurting yourself, hoping and believing that you won't, you must have some level of trust or belief that the individual will catch you.

The same is true in our relationship with God. Sometimes we want peace, we want our mind and hearts to be at rest..to stop worrying. However, in order to experience these things, it requires one thing. Yupp, trust again.

I am reminded of Matthew 6 which talks about worrying. Starting at verse 25, Jesus begins to tell the people not to worry about eating or drinking. He reminds them that their Heavenly Father will provide.

When we trust the Provider, when we learn to trust that God will protect us, catch us, and care for us, peace is available to us.

Reflect

Am I lacking peace currently?

Do I trust that God will provide?

Would I "fall" into His arms?

Prayer:

Lord, I have struggled to feel peace lately. If I am honest, I feel tense and worry often. Lord I want to experience the rest you talk about in scripture. I want to be able to fully trust that you will provide for me and you will catch me. Help me to trust you in a greater way Lord.

It's in your name I pray. Amen.

| 34 |

Not my future

The other day as I was listening to Maverick City Music's song titled, "Fear is not my Future," I began to think about my clients. I began to reflect on how many times I see discouraged, frustrated, or hopeless clients who believe that their circumstances will never change. The "but this" or "but that" comments echo in my ears from clients that see no possible way out, no change, or no solution.

As I stood there listening to the song, I just felt this nudge...this desire for my clients to know that their present situation does not have to be their future. I once stood in their shoes. I once believed that the situations I found myself in were how my life would be. That I would always be depressed. That I would always feel hopeless. But today I can say that those things were not my future.

Fellow helper, you are not alone if you find yourself hoping that your client might just "see it." That they might believe things can change for them. You will encounter many clients who are feeling hopeless. You will encounter many clients who don't believe their circumstances will ever change. But you have a unique opportunity to go to God for them. You have a unique opportunity to believe for them. This is one of the great joys of being a Christian and a therapist. We get to go to God on behalf of our clients.

So today, let's believe for our clients. Let's believe that the family dynamics can change. Let's believe that they will be able to manage their addiction. Let's believe they will experience joy again. Let's go to God for them.

We can engage in various interventions and techniques to help instill hope but above all that, we must remember that God is the ultimate giver of hope.

Prayer:

Lord, thank you for the opportunity to counsel those in my care. Thank you for choosing me to step into their situation and be light. God, would you help my clients who are feeling discouraged to believe that [insert thing] is not their future? Would you help them to see a different perspective, a possible solution, and that change is not impossible? Move in their lives Lord. Do what only you can do.

It's in your name I pray. Amen.

| 35 |

God of today

"Jesus Christ is the same yesterday and today and forever."
- Hebrews 13:8

Have you ever read the Bible and just found yourself amazed at all the things that happened in the past? From God parting the Red Sea to Jesus healing a paralyzed man and restoring a man's sight. I often try to place myself in each moment as if I am witnessing what is happening. A fly on the wall, if you will.

Well, one day Holy Spirit had to remind me that the same God who accomplished these things is still alive and active today. The healing and victories that occurred then, still happen today, they just may look different.

Just as God brought hope to Hagar when she was hopeless and discouraged *(Genesis 16)*, He can restore hope to you.

Just as God strengthened Jeremiah as he delivered difficult messages to Judah *(Jeremiah 20)*, He can give you His strength when your burden feels to heavy to carry.

Just as Jesus supplied food to those who were starving *(Matthew 15)*, He can supply your every need and more.

Just as Jesus restored health to a women who bled for years *(Luke 8)*, He can restore health and wholeness to you according to his plan.

He is not just God in the Bible, He is God with us today.

Hold this close to your heart and remember that time has not changed who He is, nor has it changed His ability to move in your life, your families life, nor your clients life.

<u>Reflect:</u>

How have I seen God move lately?

| 36 |

Never leave

Be strong and courageous. Do not be afraid or terrified because of them, for the Lord your God goes with you; he will <u>never leave you nor forsake you</u>." - Deuteronomy 31:6

No situation or circumstance will ever cause God to leave you fellow helper.

When you are faced with trouble, He will never leave you.
When you are discouraged, He will never leave you.
When you don't know what to do, He will never leave you.
When you are surrounded by darkness, He will never leave you.
When things feel chaotic in your life, He will never leave you.
When you feel restless and weary, He will never leave you.
When you can't seem to get out of bed, He will never leave you.
When you feel defeated, He will never leave you.
When you feel alone, He will never leave you.
When you feel lost and need direction, He will never leave you.

It's easy to forget this promise when what is in front of us feels so big and so powerful. However, unlike man, God does not lie or make false promises to His children. **Never is an absolute. It means at no time in the past or in the future. It means not at all.**

When you are standing in a storm and life is overwhelming, don't forget that this is God's promise fellow helper. He is always with you and never leaving you. Remind your soul this truth. Remind your client who believes in God this truth.

Hold it close to your heart, because the storms will come and you will feel that He is not present, but He is. He always is.

Practice

1. Find a comfortable position.
2. Close your eyes and take a few deep breaths.
3. Bring to mind a recent circumstance that has troubled you. Something that may have hurt you or discouraged you. Picture yourself in that moment - where you are, what you are doing, how you are feeling.
4. Take a few deep breaths as you imagine God stepping into your situation. Imagine Him kneeling down beside you and wrapping His arms around you. Breathe deeply as you imagine this.
5. Relax your body. Let his presence soothe you. Let any feelings arise. Feel the moment.
6. Imagine Him gently whisper that He is with you.
7. Stay here as long as you like - allowing God to comfort you.
8. When you are ready open your eyes and take a few more deep breaths - bringing awareness back to the present.

| 37 |

Hope deferred

A simple definition of hope is, "a feeling of expectation and desire for a certain thing to happen." Hope can be a beautiful thing. It can also be a painful thing.

We have all hoped for something in our lives. Maybe we are hoping for something at this exact moment. When we hope for something, sometimes we can feel that longing in our chest. The thing we are hoping for hasn't come true. The thing we are hoping for is seemingly delayed or deferred.

The Bible states in Proverbs 13:12, *"Hope deferred makes the heart sick, but a longing fulfilled is a tree of life."*

It's the waiting that can make you feel sick. You wonder, you question, you worry if the thing you want will ever happen. You want to hold on to hope believing for "it" but maybe doubt starts to set in. I see you. I hear you. It hurts fellow helper.

Isaiah 30:18 says, *"so the Lord must wait for you to come to Him so He can show you His love and compassion. For the Lord is a faithful God. Blessed are those who wait for His help."*

While I can't predict the how long, why, or even when of our waiting seasons, I do know that relief comes when I go to God. When I begin to acknowledge that His way and His plan is greater, I find relief. When my heart is sick from a hope deferred, I find my rest in Him. Not by doing things my way. Not by trying to figure it out. But seeking God.

Read: Isaiah 55: 8-12

When your heart feels sick from a hope deferred...

When the family member's health condition hasn't changed...

When the client hasn't gotten better...

When the desire for marriage has gone unfulfilled...

When the prospects for a new job are slim...

When you want your marriage to be restored...

When you desire to start a family...

Run to the one who listens and always has a plan. Run to the great Physician.

| 38 |

Tired

"Tired." A term I'm sure you are familiar with fellow helper.

As I sit here and type this, my heart is aching. My heart is tired. I am tired. Tired of pouring and pouring and pouring. Only to feel depleted. Some days, I want to leave work, turn off my phone, and just rest in silence. I don't want to respond to anyone. I don't want to talk to anyone. I just need a moment. I'm too tired.

It's not that I don't like or love my job. It's not that I don't enjoy this work of counseling. It's just that I have nothing else left to give. Nothing.

What I have learned and want to share with you is that it is okay to find yourself tired sometimes. As a helper, we have a delicate job that may ask a lot of us. As difficult as it may be to step away, we are no good for anyone if we are feeling empty and depleted trying to pour from an empty cup.

You simply cannot give what you do not have in your possession.

So today, if you find yourself like me...tired. Exhausted. Depleted. Empty. I encourage you to step away. Take a day or two. Silence your phone. Lay in bed. Get with God. Just as you prioritize your clients, take time to prioritize yourself. Take time to get the refill you need.

The inner voice will tell you that you have to show up and you can't cancel on those clients. But you can. And this is your permission to do so.

Read: Matthew 11:28-30

<u>**Check in:**</u>

How am I feeling?

How's my cup looking?

| 39 |

I believe in you

There are many things I would love to go back and tell the younger version of myself, however if I had to choose 1, I think I would tell her to believe in herself. I would tell her that she is capable of far more than she thinks and she is equipped by God to do the work He has led her to.

One night as I was watching season 2 of Netflix's "*Is it cake?*" I saw this younger version of me. I saw a young baker who doubted her ability to create the cake she selected. She jokingly stated that she was going to be sent home because of who she was competing against. While I imagine she was slightly joking, I also believe there was some truth to her statement. She didn't believe that she was good enough for the work in front of her. I have shared her sentiments. I too, have believed that I wasn't good enough or capable to do this work. I too doubted myself.

This devotional was birthed out of that doubt. This devotional is a reminder that we are equipped for this. It's a reminder to myself and to you, to believe in the gifts given to us. So let's take time today to rest in that...

<u>Engage:</u>

Take a moment to find a mirror. Once you do so, think of what encouragement you need to hear today. Take it a step further and place your hand over your heart and affirm yourself.

Example: [Insert name] YOU are amazing. You have such a heart for this field and the work that you do. You ARE equipped for this. God has equipped you for this. You are capable and I believe in you.

Whether you need it now or the younger version of yourself needs it, believe in yourself fellow helper.

Reflect:

What would I tell the younger version of myself?

| 40 |

Pass it on

I vividly remember a time in college where a person I knew was going through a really tough time. I wanted to encourage him somehow so I had sent him a little quote image talking about how a plant grows through dirt and we also grow through our experiences.

I don't know if that little image did much for him but the moment sticks with me to this day.

We have all grown through something. We all have stories or memories of moments in our life that were rough. But what do we do with those memories? Do we just leave them in the past and keep it moving? Well....we could. However, I don't believe that is what God wants to happen. I believe that He desires for us to pass it on. To testify about it.

As Christians we might hear that word testify or testimony often. Simply put, it means to tell the story. To tell of what God has done.

After having an encounter with Jesus, the woman at the well went to testify in her town (John 4:1-26, 39-42). After persecuting Christians for years, Saul (later called Paul), went on to testify and spread the gospel throughout the world (Acts 22:1-21).

You see, the "dirt" we experience in this life, God wants to use. The challenging seasons, the heartbreak, the hard times that God has brought us through...are to be used.

While your client may never know what God has done in your life, you have a unique vantage point from your experiences. You may have tools, lessons, and hope from those seasons in your life that can help your client. You have things to pass on to those around you.

This may look different for us considering many factors such as the setting, professionalism, beliefs, and ethics. However remember that self-disclosure can be an effective tool when used appropriately.

I have had clients I've had the privilege of sharing portions of my story with and seen it positively impact the therapeutic relationship and provide hope to the client, because I felt led to "pass it on."

<u>Reflection:</u>

With God, nothing is ever wasted.

What has God brought me through that I may need to "pass on?"

What tools or lessons have I learned that may help someone else?

Prayer

Hey Lord, today I am in need of some encouragement. I need just a little reminder that I am doing what pleases you. Lord it is far and few that I get to hear outcomes or truly know the impact that I make on clients. And while I don't necessarily need that feedback, Lord it is helpful to be reminded that the work I do is not in vain.

Lord I pray that you would help me to be encouraged today. Would you show me that you are using me. Whether that be through your sweet presence and comfort in session. Through a client's feedback. Or some other form.

Lord your Word says, "Ask and it will be given to you; seek and you will find; knock and the door will be opened to you." Father I am asking. I am seeking. Show me that I am capable of counseling those in my care. Show me that this work is meaningful. Lord meet me today.

Lord you are worthy and I thank you that with you, I don't have to live in discouragement. I thank you that with you I can stand on the truth that you have hope, plans, and future you have for me.

Thank you Lord.
It's in your name I pray. Amen.

| 41 |

Heartache

Have you ever felt that deep heartache? That sinking in your chest? It's like this uncomfortable feeling that no stretch, medicine, shaking, or deep breathing will move. I've felt that. I feel it now as I write. But what I also feel is peace. Though my heart aches and I just don't understand the circumstances I am in...I have peace.

That doesn't mean it doesn't hurt because it does. That doesn't mean I don't have questions because I do.

But I do know that God is near, He loves me deeply, and there is purpose in my pain that is beyond my understanding.

Fellow helper, we cannot control nor predict the things that may unfold in our lives or our client's lives. We have no idea what the next year, day, hour, or minute may hold. However what we do know with certainty, is that *"the LORD is close to the brokenhearted and saves those who are crushed in spirit"* (Psalm 34:18).

When our/our client's spirit is crushed...
When our/our client's is broken and aching...
When our/our client's world is thrown off...
When our/our client's mind is spinning...
God is near.

And because He is near, peace can exist even in the midst of your heartache. But as we navigate our pain, we must draw near too.

Reflect:
How does this truth comfort me?
How might this help a client?

Prayer:
Lord I thank you that you are near to me. In times of heartbreak, in times of struggle, in times of uncertainty, you are near. [This] hurts right now but I know that I'm going to make it through. I know this is not the end. I know it will get better. But right now, I bring my pain to you. I don't know how long this will hurt but you are the mighty comforter and my pain is safe with you. You will comfort me in this and for that I thank you. I thank you that this pain has a purpose. Lord I am drawing near to you help me today.

| 42 |

"I can't"

"I have come to believe that caring for myself is not self-indulgent. Caring for myself is an act of survival."
— Audre Lorde

Have you ever felt guilty for needing a day off? Have you ever felt wrong for canceling on your clients? I know I have. It went something like this:

I can't take today off, my clients expect me to be there.
I don't feel well, but I can't cancel all my appointments.
I feel exhausted, but I can make it to Friday.
I need to schedule this appointment, but I can't cancel on them.

Early on in my career, these were some of the thoughts that went through my head. I didn't want to cancel appointments. I had to show up no matter what. If I felt sick, of course I stayed home, but even then I felt guilty for canceling.

What I soon realized is that I was neglecting my own needs. I must have thought I was superhuman, free from any limitations. I'll be fine, I'd tell myself. I was so focused on my clients and what I believed they needed, that I didn't take a day when I needed it.

But as the quote above suggests, caring for yourself is a means of survival fellow helper. We are not superhuman. Eventually we will crash.

And I'll end with this story: One day, my supervisor said something to me along the lines of…Your client's have made it this far without you, trust that they know how to figure things out. She didn't mean it in a harsh way, but rather she wanted me to trust the process and know that it was okay if I had to miss or cancel a session.

So today's reminder is this: Do what you need to take care of yourself.

Even though we may feel like we can't cancel, we can and maybe we should… so let's practice this when needed.

| 43 |

God's chosen instrument

Saul persecuted Christians...until one day he didn't. Saul's story can be found in the book of Acts and from what we are told, this man was not one that you wanted to encounter, especially if you were a follower of Jesus (Acts 8:1-3; 9:1-2).

Later in the text the Bible tells us, *"Saul spent several days with the disciples in Damascus. At once he began to preach in the synagogues that Jesus is the Son of God. All those who heard him were astonished and asked, "Isn't he the man who raised havoc in Jerusalem among those who call on this name? And hasn't he come here to take them as prisoners to the chief priests?" Yet Saul grew more and more powerful and baffled the Jews living in Damascus by proving that Jesus is the Messiah"* (Acts 9:19-22).

God chose Saul and transformed him (Acts 9:15). He was God's chosen instrument to reach people and make His name known.

Saul's conversion reminds us that no one is beyond the reach of God. God can use us greatly - irregardless of our past.

Fellow helper, you are God's chosen instrument to reach certain clients, certain family members, and certain people in life. I hope that fact alone encourages you.

Whether you are new to this field, considering this field, or seasoned, as you remain connected to God, He can use you in a mighty way to transform lives. Just let that settle in for a second.

He wants to use YOU.

It's a beautiful thing to know that God still uses us even though we are less than perfect beings. I am certainly grateful for that!

<u>Truth for today:</u>

I am God's chosen instrument. He equipped me for this.

| 44 |

Ask

When in doubt...always ask.

This is something I have held onto working in this profession. When I began my first full time position as a therapist, I was insecure, riddled with imposter syndrome, and had a lot of doubt. So much so that I was often afraid to ask for assistance from anyone. I didn't want people to think I didn't know what I was doing. *How could I forget something that I know I learned in graduate school? How could I not remember the criteria for borderline personality disorder? What is a TDO?*

I often sat mute in meetings silently questioning the discussion and then spent time googling various things when I returned to my office.

Do you resonate at all? Maybe you hesitate to consult with a coworker because you fear "looking stupid?" Maybe you nod in agreement with someone to appear as if you know what they are talking about? Maybe you sit quietly in meetings afraid that if you speak up people may think less of you?

Whatever the case may be, I quickly learned that it is better to ask than make a mistake because I pretended to know. I had to put my pride aside and what I believed my colleagues might think of me.

No clinician has all of the knowledge, latest research, diagnostic criteria all memorized fellow helper. No clinician remembers every single thing taught in graduate school. This is something I wished I was told as a young clinician entering my first full time position. I didn't have to be perfect but I should consult or ask questions.

Today I pray for you fellow helper. If you find that you have difficulty consulting or asking questions, I pray that you would begin to experience an openness to seeking out guidance. That you would release the pressure of having to know it all.

<u>Truth for today:</u>

I don't know it all, but I can ask. And I am still equipped for this.

| 45 |

Equipped

Hey fellow helper, repeat after me:

I am equipped to help those around me.
If I take medication for my own mental health concerns, I am
still equipped.
If I have my own therapist, I am still equipped.
If I struggle with my own mental health, I am still equipped.
If I have to seek support from others, I am still equipped.
If I have been diagnosed with a disorder, I am still equipped.
If I have a bad day, I am still equipped.
If I feel "off," I am still equipped.

My circumstances and conditions to do not disqualify me
from being called to do this work.
My God calls and qualifies me to do this work.

I am not a perfect helper.
I am not immune to difficulties and challenges.
And I am not any less worthy to care for people if any of
these things are true.

I am equipped for this.
I choose to believe this truth today.

| 46 |

You deserve

Hey fellow helper,

Daily you work diligently to make sure your clients feel safe, supported, heard, celebrated, etc. Daily you create a safe place for your clients. It's not surprising that you may want the same in return.

I think every person longs some of these things in their relationships whether they know it or not...but as a helper, I believe that this desire may be magnified. It makes sense. This can be a lonely job. Especially if you find yourself working solo in private practice.

But for the one who needs it today....this desire isn't "wrong." It's real and I see you.

You too, are deserving of spaces you feel seen. You too, are deserving of spaces to be heard and listened too. You too, are deserving of spaces you feel safe. You too, are deserving of spaces to be open and vulnerable.

Reflection:

Do I feel seen and heard in my relationships?
Who are the people in my life that I can trust?

Truth for today:

I am deserving of safe spaces too.

| 47 |

Intercession

As therapists, we have a unique opportunity to intercede for our clients. I love this because whether they know God or not, we still have an opportunity to submit requests to God on their behalf.

When I think of the word intercede, I think of stepping in. I think of speaking up for someone.

A simple definition from vocabulary.com says that intercession is "prayer or petition in favor of someone else."

I am reminded of Aaron and his son's duties in the Old Testament. Aaron was deemed the high priest and had a specific job to go to God on behalf of the Israelites to atone for their sins through various sacrifices. He had access to God that the people did not. He and his sons could enter the Tabernacle as priests called by God. They were intercessors. People who went to God on behalf of the people. This was prior to the birth of The High Priest who would enter the scene years later – Jesus. Jesus paid the ultimate price by dying on the Christ on our behalf for our sins. He is the supreme example.

Fellow helper, because of our relationship with God and our unique access to our clients, we too can practice intercession. We should practice it. Going to God continuously for our clients. Interceding for their healing, for their relief, for their families, and their situations.

Intercession isn't something that only certain people can do. It is something that we all have the ability to practice.

Scripture:

"And pray in the Spirit on all occasions with all kinds of prayers and requests. With this in mind, be alert and always keep on praying for all the Lord's people." - Ephesians 6:18

Truth for today:

I am an intercessor and there is power in going to God on behalf of my clients.

| 48 |

Miracles

The Lord said to Moses, "How long will these people treat me with contempt? How long will they refuse to believe in me, in spite of all the signs I have performed among them?
- Numbers 14:11

God is truly a Man of patience. If you don't believe me, just take some time and read through the books of Exodus, Leviticus, and Numbers. The Israelites were slaves in Egypt for 430 years and God eventually used two men named Moses and Aaron to lead the Israelites out of Egypt (Exodus 12). The Israelites were then headed to "a land flowing with milk and honey." A land promised by God in Exodus 3:17. However, a series of events happened along the way. The Israelites engaged in a lot of sin, they complained, they disobeyed the Lord, and so much more.

I'll be the first to admit, I got tired of hearing their complaints. Time and time again God provided for them, He protected them against their enemies, He performed many signs, He went with them. Yet they constantly grumbled against Moses saying that it would have been "better" for them to stay in Egypt (Numbers 14:2).

Despite all the signs God had shown them, they still lacked confidence in what the Lord would do for them.

I think many times, we can be like the Israelites. We forget all that God has done in our lives and doubt what He can do.

Let's consider it in a clinical lens: we forget the clients that experienced healing during their time in counseling. We forget the healing God allowed to happen in our lives. We forgot the ways that He brought us clients and filled our caseloads. We forget the ways that He worked out a situation in our favor.

If God has done something once, He can absolutely do it again fellow helper. It may not always look the same, but just as He has done miracles in the past, He does them today.

Reflect:

What miracles has God done in my life?
What miracles have I been able to witness in my clients' lives, friends' lives, or my family?

Truth for today:

God does miracles today. I have confidence in His miracle-working power.

| 49 |

God's design

One of my favorite things to do, specifically in the fall, is to drive down the interstate and just admire the beauty in each tree, the colors, the various types. It's breathtaking in my opinion. God is so creative in that way. God is also creative in how He uniquely designed us.

Ephesians 2:10 says, *"For we are God's handiwork, created in Christ Jesus to do good works, which God prepared in advance for us to do." Some versions describe us as "His workmanship" or "His masterpiece."*

Simply put, He made us to be a certain way.

Have you ever stopped to consider how God created a client? Have you ever stopped to ask God to help you understand how He uniquely designed someone? What may work best? *Neither have I.*

It sounds like an odd thing to ask God but He placed it on my heart one day as I reflected on my day and my work with a particular client I couldn't fully conceptualize.

But God is the ultimate designer. Could you imagine what you'd learn by sitting with the Creator and allowing Him to speak about His creation (aka your clients)?

Fellow helper, I believe that He is inviting us to ask. I believe He wants to supply us with insight into His unique design so we may best help our clients. So let's ask.

<u>**Reflect:**</u>

How might asking God help me understand how He created a client transform my work with them?

<u>**Truth for today:**</u>

God has created each of my clients. As I seek Him, He will equip me to work with each of them.

"Just keep going"

Watching the Netflix show *Is it Cake,* has been very insightful and emotional for me. I really wish I could be a judge and taste those cakes! However, what often gets me is the goodbyes and the victories.

As I watched the top 5 compete for a spot in the finales, there was a moment that stood out to me. One of the bakers was behind on her cake. She had little time to finish the final details that would trick the judges. The baker begins to cry and tells herself to "just keep going." Mind you, her cake looks completely different than the decoy items.

Fast forward to the round where the judges have to guess which one is her cake, guess what happens? One of the judges confidently says, "it's not number 2," which was indeed the cake. They did not find her cake. The baker began to cry. She fooled the judges.

As the show continued, a line in Deitrick Haddon's song "He's able" emerged in my mind: "Don't give up on God, cause He won't give up on you. He's able."

In this moment I was reminded that even when our circumstance don't look favorable, God can move. He doesn't give up on us...

Maybe you are worried about your business and lacking revenue. Maybe you are burnt out and tired of your job. Maybe you haven't been able to pass your licensure exam despite all your studying. Maybe you can't find a suitable job.

I share with you the same encouragement that the baker whispered as tears rolled down her face: "just keep going."

When I say just keep going, I mean…don't stop believing. Don't stop praying. Don't give up on yourself. He alone is able to do what seems unfavorable, unlikely, impossible. It might not always look how we imagined, but He will move.

Scripture:

For with God nothing shall be impossible. - Luke 1:37

Prayer:

God you make the impossible possible. According to Isaiah 43:19, you make ways in the wilderness and rivers in the dessert. You are able to do things that I cannot. Lord help me to rest in this truth today. It's in your name I pray. Amen.

Prayer

Hi God,

If I am being honest it's taking everything in me to get out of bed this morning. The thought of going to work is daunting. It's exhausting. I feel like I can't move. Like I can't bring myself to get up. My thoughts overwhelm me.

God, Isaiah 40:29 says that you give power to the weak and strength to the powerless. Would you to help me today? Please. I could really use some strength. I can't do this work on my own Father. I can't do anything without you and I ask that you would forgive me for trying.

I need you Lord. Please help me.
Strengthen me, guide me, hear my cry today Father.

In this moment I lift my hands and surrender my plans, my thoughts, my will, and my emotions to you.
I give you everything and ask in return that you would allow me to experience your strength.

Please give me energy and motivation to do the work that you need me to do today.
Give me joy and power to get up.
I love you and I need you Lord.
Amen.

| 51 |

A Word from God

Close your eyes and take 3-4 deep breaths before reading today fellow helper.

Hear this gentle and loving whisper from God:

Abide in me.
Rest in me.
You are not the author of the story.
I am.

Take a few more deep breaths.
Gently and slowly, tell yourself:

Abide in Him.
Rest in Him.
He is the author of the story.
Not me.

Read:

John 15: 4-5

Matthew 11:28-30

Jeremiah 29:11

Truth for today:

I am equipped to do this work because I know that God is the author of every story.

| 52 |

Different

When you walk with Jesus and invite Him into your heart, you begin to look different. It's not that there is this drastic physical change, but it's almost like an inward makeover, if you will. God's light begins to live in you and shine through you.

One prayer that has stuck with me in every season of life is: God help me to be a light to those around me.

More than anything I want God to be seen, felt, and experienced. Not so that I can get the glory, but that He would. That people who don't know God, would become curious about Him.

This prayer has allowed many opportunities to share about the hope that I have. To share that my faith and relationship with Jesus is something that is very important to me. Because the truth is that people do become curious. People notice when you are kind. People notice when you genuinely care. People notice when you exhibit patience in a particularly trying situation. People notice. People watch. And on occasion, people may also ask. This includes our clients.

1 Peter 3:15-16 says, "But in your hearts revere Christ as Lord. Always be prepared to give an answer to everyone who asks you to give the reason for the hope that you have. But do this with gentleness and respect,"

Matthew 5:16 says, "In the same way, let your light shine before others, that they may see your good deeds and glorify your Father in heaven."

<u>Reflect:</u>

In what ways does your relationship with God change you?
How has your life changed because of your relationship with Him?
Do you handle things differently because of your relationship with God? In what ways?

As you think about these things, I want to remind you that you do have His light inside of you and it does makes you different fellow helper. I pray that you would allow that light to shine everywhere you go today. I pray that your clients may see and begin to know God because of His light at work in you.

<u>Truth for today:</u>

I am equipped because God's light shines in and through me.

| 53 |

Therapist + Christian

I ran across a post on Instagram where a clinician was essentially being criticized for posts about being a therapist and a Christian. On the one hand, people were claiming that she "shouldn't work" with certain clients if she is a Christian. The other group of people believed that she was imposing her beliefs on clients. This person emphasized that she chooses to show love, compassion, and empathy to everyone she works, regardless of their beliefs. She wanted to clarify that she was a therapist who identifies as Christian rather than a Christian counselor. Because the two are different.

I myself am a therapist and identify as a Christian. I work with a wide variety of clients and I imagine that many of you may come from various backgrounds as well.

As clinicians we abide by a code of ethics which urges that we "do no harm." This includes not imposing beliefs on clients.

As a therapist who is also Christian, I am able to sit with many clients because I know that regardless of their beliefs and struggles, they are a human being that is loved by Jesus.

In His time on earth Jesus spent time with both believers and nonbelievers. I personally believe that I am called to do the same. Hence why I did not choose to solely pursue an education in Biblical or Christian counseling.

Fellow helper, you will encounter many clients, some who share similar beliefs, some who share different beliefs, and some who don't have any beliefs at all, but every client is deserving of love and that's what Jesus would want us to show.

Ephesians 5:1 says, *"Imitate God, therefore, in everything you do, because you are his dear children."*

Showing love is not imposing beliefs. Caring for clients is not imposing beliefs. Being warm and compassionate is not imposing beliefs. Imposing beliefs implies that you are attempting to influence or change a client's beliefs, attitudes, feelings, or behaviors based on what you believe to be right. This is simply not our job.

Reflect:

Do I find it difficult to sit with clients that share dissimilar beliefs?

In what ways do I make sure I am not imposing beliefs on a client?

Read:

Mark 12:30-31

1 John 4:20-21

| 54 |

Why me?

Have you ever wondered why God chose Mary to birth Jesus? Have you ever wondered if Mary herself questioned, "why me?" If she ever considered why she was selected to carry the Savior of the World?

Though the Bible doesn't specifically tell us why God chose Mary, God knows why. It was a part of His plan.

One day in a staff meeting, I was sharing about a client whom requested to work with me. This was a client I had never met, never heard of, never seen. Silently I wondered, *Why me? Maybe they made a mistake? They meant to request someone else.* This small request was something that I couldn't wrap my mind around, but it was a moment that God used to encourage me.

I am reminded that like Mary, God also chooses you and I fellow helper.

Things may happen in your life that make you stop and think, 'why me.' Doors may open. Opportunities may be given to you. Clients may request you. You may help a specific individual(s) in their time of need. It is not a coincidence or happenstance. It is His plan.

Have you ever heard that saying, "God opens doors that no man can shut?" That saying is scripture, coined from Revelation 3:7. God opens doors that only you can walk through fellow helper. He chooses you for opportunities and positions that no other person could fulfill.

Let this truth encourage you today. The answer to "why me" is because God chose you.

<u>Prayer:</u>

God, thank you. Thank you for opening doors that no man can shut. Thank you for choosing me even when I don't understand. Thank you for calling me to specific places and using me to reach certain people. Thank you for thinking of me. God, I don't deserve your goodness but I am amazed and so grateful that you choose to include me in your plans.

<u>Truth for today:</u>

I am equipped because God chose me.

| 55 |

Poison

One day as I was driving by a mom-and-pop auto shop, I noticed their sign which said, "Unforgiveness is like drinking poison and expecting the other person to die."

Have you ever lived with unforgiveness in your heart? (*I know I have.*) Held a grudge towards someone who wronged you? (*Oh, yea.*) Did it help you at all? (*Didn't help me at all.*)

I have found that forgiving others is a necessary part of my healing journey. I'd suggest that it is also important for you and your clients as well.

Many times we sit with clients who are reaping the effects of unforgiveness. They experience bitterness, anger, defensiveness, envy, and more. Their blood boils as they speak of the person who wronged them. Or maybe they deny how hurt they are by that person. One thing is clear, it is negatively impacting them.

In Peter's curiosity, he asked Jesus, *"Lord, how many times shall I forgive my brother when he sins against me? Up to seven times?" Jesus answered, "I tell you, not seven times, but seventy-seven times"* (Matthew 18: 21-22).

One can infer that Jesus is teaching him that there should be no limit to forgiveness.

Depending on who you may ask, forgiveness may or may not be important however, as believers it is crucial. Forgiveness is the entire message of the gospel. It is something we are encouraged to do (Ephesians 4:32).

Maybe your client is not a believer? Research has still proven that the act of forgiveness has significant benefits. It may be helpful to explore some of that research.

Whether this resonates with you or it brings to mind a client you're working with, know that forgiveness plays a significant role in healing and growth fellow helper. Let's stay away from the poison.

Reflect:

Is there a person(s) that I need to forgive?

How has forgiving others benefitted me?

| 56 |
Who I am

You are light.
You are love.
You are kind.
You are caring.
You are worthy.
You are His.

Remember this today.

You are who God says you are, NOT what you do.

It is so easy to place our identity in other things. Whether it's media, another persons opinion, money, our job, sports, success? The list could go on.

The first part of 1 Peter 2:9 (TPT) says, *"But you are God's chosen treasure.."*

You are valuable.
You were selected.
You are His.

As a therapist, it is important to remember WHO you are in Christ.

Therapy is what you do, it is not your identity.

Sometimes we may need to step back and evaluate or reevaluate where our identity is placed. Today could be a good day to do so.

<u>Truth for today:</u>

I am equipped for this because my identity is in Christ.

Seeds

"I planted the seed in your hearts, and Apollos watered it, but it was God who made it grow. It's not important who does the planting, or who does the watering. What's important is that God makes the seed grow."
- 1 Corinthians 3:6-7

Have you ever had a client who dropped out of therapy?
A client who had to move away?
A client who appeared to be making progress and then seemingly disappeared?
A client who ended therapy earlier than you would have recommended?

In each of these cases we might be left with many questions, yet we rarely get those answers. I struggled with this for a long time. *Was it me? Did I offend them? Are they okay?* I would reflect on our last interactions as if that was helpful and would somehow give me the answer I was longing for. *Was I having a bad day?* Eventually this grew to be tiring.

As I reflect on this scripture, I begin to acknowledge that perhaps that is the way God intended it to be. Perhaps God only intended for us to encounter a client for a specific amount of time. Perhaps God needed us to meet with them in a specific season or particular moment. Perhaps God used us to plant a small seed in their lives or water what was previously planted by someone else. We could consider a million different possibilities, yet the truth remains that we will never actually know.

In these moments, we get to choose what we will believe fellow helper. While we may hope that we never offend someone, it does happen and it is a possibility. However, in other cases, we can choose to stand on this scripture. We can choose to believe that even though so and so dropped out of therapy or moved away, we have planted or watered a seed in their lives that God will grow. Because that's what matters.

Prayer:

God, I am worried because [insert client] dropped out of therapy. While I may never know what happened, I pray that a seed was planted or watered. God I release the unknown. I release the outcome. Help me to trust that you have them in your hands.

| 58 |

The Well

When a Samaritan woman came to draw water, Jesus said to her, "Will you give me a drink?" (His disciples had gone into the town to buy food.) The Samaritan woman said to him, "You are a Jew and I am a Samaritan woman. How can you ask me for a drink?" (For Jews do not associate with Samaritans.) Jesus answered her, "If you knew the gift of God and who it is that asks you for a drink, you would have asked him and he would have given you living water." "Sir," the woman said, "you have nothing to draw with and the well is deep. Where can you get this living water? Are you greater than our father Jacob, who gave us the well and drank from it himself, as did also his sons and his livestock?" Jesus answered, "Everyone who drinks this water will be thirsty again, but whoever drinks the water I give them will never thirst. Indeed, the water I give them will become in them a spring of water welling up to eternal life." The woman said to him, "Sir, give me this water so that I won't get thirsty and have to keep coming here to draw water." – John 4:7-15

One day God gave me this image of a woman sitting at a fountain on the campus of a job I had applied for. She had black circles around her eyes and looked depleted. I had just applied for the job but hadn't yet been offered a position. 3 years later, I am still at this job and this image continues to surface every now and then.

This image that I saw reminds me of the Samaritan woman at the well. A woman who was tired, thirsty, and depleted was sitting by the fountain (or a well in the case of the Samaritan woman) looking to fulfill her thirst. What God reminded me was that only He can satisfy that thirst. Hence why He told the Samaritan women, "whoever drinks the water I give them will never thirst."

I believe that God was reminding me that He was my source. He was my well of living water. The woman at the fountain represented me. The location of the fountain represented the job I was going to take. His warning to me was that I may feel depleted and tired in the job but I must remember to always come back to Him. For only He can satisfy.

In moments where we feel exhausted, tired, and just "done," it may be that we need to fall on our knees and worship. To cry out and draw from God.

Fellow helper, God is the well of Living water. In other words He is our sustenance. With Him we are nourished and capable of much. Apart from Him we experience dehydration and depletion. We cannot afford to do this work apart from Him.

Song for further encouragement:
"Only you can satisfy" by William McDowell

Truth for Today:
I am equipped for this because God is my well of Living water.

| 59 |

God of Comfort

When you think about comfort what comes to mind? Is it a hug? Is it your favorite weighted blanket? A warm cup of tea? God?

For a long time, I struggled with the concept of God being a comforter. *How can God comfort me when He isn't physically present? How can I truly experience His comfort?*

What I have since learned is that God's comfort may not always be in the form of a physical means like we hope or imagine, but God provides a comfort that quiets our restless spirit. It's a comfort that brings peace to chaos, calm to worry, and hope to weariness. I think the Apostle Paul knew this very well. Consider his words in 2 Corinthians 1:3-4:

"Praise be to the God and Father of our Lord Jesus Christ, the Father of compassion and the God of all comfort, who comforts us in all our troubles, so that we can comfort those in any trouble with the comfort we ourselves receive from God. For just as we share abundantly in the sufferings of Christ, so also our comfort abounds through Christ."

If we look at Paul's life, he was imprisoned for some time during his ministry. Not only this but he suffered quite a lot in his life for Christ. Nonetheless, his circumstances didn't stop him from writing letters of encouragement to groups of Christians. He was comforted.

In moments of unease, worry, and restlessness, remember that God's comfort is available to you, fellow helper. Call out to Him and ask Him to comfort you. And if you find that you also long for the physical comfort, cling to His Word, literally. I have found that squeezing my Bible tightly often feels like a hug from God. So hug Him today. Experience His comfort.

Truth for today:

I am equipped for this because God comforts me.

Prayer

Today I told a client that I wouldn't give up on them. Those words I uttered were only from God. They weren't planned, they just flowed. The client smiled, appearing relieved, because so many doctors, clinicians, and others had. And as I think about my words to this client, I can't help but be reminded of how God doesn't give up on us.

Lord, today we thank you that you are with us. When life feels dark, painful, and uncertain, you don't give up on us. We can't always see you, feel you, or hear you, but you are there. And this is so hard to fathom or believe at times God but thank you that you see us as worthy. Your Word tells us that you leave the 99 for the 1. So even when we stray, you follow. You never give up. When people have given up on us, you never do.

Father, sometimes I feel as though you have left me. Sometimes I believe that you have given up on me. Lord would you remind me today of your immense love for me and your relentless pursuit of me. For both myself and for my clients, would you allow us to experience your loving presence. Your warm embrace. Would you help us believe that you are near. That you are with us even though you seem so so far away.

Thank you that you don't give up on us Father. Even when we might give up on you, nothing we do can ever make us unlovable in your eyes. Thank you Father that you always stay. Allow us to hide this truth in our heart today and every day thereafter. We love you Father, Amen.

<u>Song for further encouragement:</u>

The God Who Stays - Matthew West

| 60 |

Start with God

Every morning I start my day off either by listening to worship music, prayer, reading my Bible, or some combination of these things. It's become a consistent habit over the years.

Starting my day with God isn't just something I want to do it's also something that I have to do. First thing in the morning, my mind begins to think about all the things on my list for the day. I think about what I will wear, what I will eat, what I will pack for lunch, what I need to do after work. Sometimes this can lead to dread as I try to get my day going.

By turning on worship music, praying, or reading my Bible, I begin to center my mind on encouraging and helpful things. I feel energized and geared up to start my day.

I think about athletes who often have a pre-game warmup and playlist they listen to. They are "getting their mind right" in order to play their best game. As Christians, this is essentially what we are also doing.

The moment we leave our home, we are entering a battle. There are many things that can effect us when we leave the home and I have recognized that the mindset I start my day often influences how I respond to things. It influences how I respond to the driver riding my tail, how I respond to a challenging client, how I respond to my coworkers, and how I feel about my caseload or tasks for the day.

The bottomline is that when we invite God into our day, first thing in the morning, it has the ability to change things. It has the ability to change our mindset and change us, as we enter a new day.

While prayer, reading the Bible, or listening to worship music are my personal go-to's, there are many ways we can start our day with God. If you don't already, consider how you can do so today fellow helper.

<u>Reflect:</u>

How do I currently start my day?

What can I do to start my day with God?

How might starting my day with God be helpful for me?

<u>Read:</u>

Psalm 143:8

| 61 |

For the Lord

Colossians 3:23-24 says, *"Whatever you do, work at it with all your heart, as working for the Lord, not for human masters, since you know that you will receive an inheritance from the Lord as a reward. It is the Lord Christ you are serving."*

I use to keep this verse taped to my desk when I started my first "big girl" job out of college. For me, it was a reminder that the work that I do is to please the Lord. It was a daily reminder to check my motives and acknowledge who I was ultimately working for. Yes I wanted good performance evaluations to keep my job, but I knew that the work I was doing served a greater purpose.

The same is true as we work with our various clients and colleagues. The way we counsel our clients should honor the Lord. The way we speak and interact with our colleagues should honor the Lord. The way we show up to work should honor the Lord. Everything we do, should honor the Lord.

As you consider the work you do, whether it be a 9 to 5 office job, you are strictly remote, or some other variation, in what ways do you honor the Lord in what you do? In what ways do you find yourself working for the Lord and not man?

When we work for the Lord two things happen: 1)we ultimately please God and 2) we prosper and receive His blessings along the way.

<u>Prayer:</u>

God I thank you today for the job that you have given me.
Though it may not be the perfect position, I'm thankful that it
takes care of me (and my family too). Lord I ask that every
day as I prepare to sit down with clients, interact with my
colleagues, and show up for work, you would get the glory.
Allow my words, my actions, my thoughts, be pleasing to you.
Remind me that the work I do is for you, not for man. Amen.

<u>Truth for today:</u>

I am equipped for this because the work I do is for the Lord.

| 62 |

Life is "lifing"

Have you ever sat at the beach and just watched the waves gently dissolve onto the shore? Watched the sun rise over the ocean? It's one of the most peaceful experiences. It's why the beach is one of my favorite places to escape to. It brings this calming presence over me.

Recently I've heard several people in my life mention that "life is lifing." I knew exactly what they meant without having to ask. It means that life is happening and it's almost as if you have no control. When "life is lifing" things just continue to happen. You can't catch a break.

What I have learned is that when life is lifing, I must cling to peace. I must find a sense of calm. Trying to gain control won't do. Sometimes it means turning of the tv, sitting and breathing, resting, or closing your eyes. Sometimes it means sitting in silence. Sometimes it means watching the waves gently dissolve onto the shore. It means finding your calm.

Isaiah 26:33 says, *"You will keep in perfect peace the mind that is dependent on you, for it is trusting in you."*

Sitting here at my office desk typing, I feel God's calming presence. Though life is happening all around me and to me, I still feel calm because I know that He is in control even when I am not. I am able to be present in sessions, experience a sense of calm, and be my authentic self, though the waves are a bit rough.

Fellow helper, if you too feel that "life is lifing," I encourage you to remember the waves. To find Peace. Waves will come and sometimes they may throw us off balance but in due time, the waves will dissolve and a break will come.

<u>Reflect:</u>

Where do I find the most peace?

What have I found helpful in times where" life is lifing"?

| 63 |

A heavy load

"He gives strength to the weary and increases the power of the weak. Even youths grow tired and weary, and young men stumble and fall; but those who hope in the Lord will renew their strength. They will soar on wings like eagles; they will run and not grow weary, they will walk and not be faint."
– Isaiah 40:29-31 NIV

If you've ever lifted weights, you might have experienced a point in your workout where your muscles are fatigued and you begin to shake as you try to complete just one more rep. You're giving every last ounce of strength that you have to complete that bench press. I've experienced this countless times and thankfully it has never backfired on me haha.

It's generally recommended that you have a spotter while bench pressing. This is someone who can help lift the weight in case your muscles give out or something else happens. It's not always necessary but it's helpful to prevent accidents.

We often lift heavy weights in life. Whether it be the work that we do or in our lives outside of work, we too can get exhausted from lifting heavy loads. We too can become weary and weak. However the good news is that we have a personal spotter available to us 24/7.

God is our spotter. He is our strength when we are weak. When we are tired and don't think we can take anymore,

He is there to take the load. Scripture constantly reminds us of this. Scripture tells us that God is not only able to lift the heavy burdens, but He desires to take it from us.

As you allow God to take your heavy loads, He will renew and restore your strength fellow helper. As you look to Him and seek Him, the weight won't crush you. Call out to your spotter to take the heavy load.

<u>Read:</u>

Isaiah 46:4

Matthew 11:28-30

Psalm 46:1-3

<u>Truth for today:</u>

I am equipped for this because I give God my heavy loads.

| 64 |

Joy is coming

"Weeping may last through the night, but joy comes with the morning."
-Psalm 30:5b

Have you ever heard someone use the idiom, "I see the light at the end of the tunnel?" Or maybe used it yourself?

Typically it is used when someone can see signs that a tough situation might be coming to an end. They can see that the end is near.

I've heard many clients say this as they describe coming out of a season of depression. Their mood was improving. The motivation was slowly finding its way back. Maybe they were smiling a little more. Finding themselves enjoying activities once again. Feeling a bit lighter. They could see the light.

As helpers, we too can find ourselves stuck in the tunnel. We too can find ourselves yearning for the light at the end. Maybe you've been in a tough season at work and you are anxiously anticipating a break. Maybe you've been struggling in your private practice. Maybe you've been wrestling with a personal matter.

Whatever season you might find yourself in fellow helper, I want to encourage you with the words of the psalmist: your weeping may last for a night but joy is coming.

Joy *IS* coming. Not was, not might, not will possibly come. Joy is coming with certainty.

Keep pressing and seeking God in whatever season you find yourself in fellow helper, trusting that that morning will come. Trusting that He will bring you out of the tunnel and into His light. Things will one day be better and joy will come.

Read:

Ecclesiastes 3:1-8

John 16:33

Reflect:

What has God brought me through in the past?

What beliefs, thoughts, or views are currently interfering with my ability to trust that joy will come?

| 65 |

The "helper hat"

As a helper, you sit with clients daily providing care, offering a safe space, and lending your ear. This is something you love to do. It's something you have dedicated time, money, and focus to developing and growing in your craft. Time in school, time reading the latest research, time attending conferences and professional development opportunities, time planning for sessions.

However, in our quest to be the best helpers that we can be, we must not neglect the necessary time to also sit with ourselves and receive. We must not forget to take off the helper hat every now and then.

I am reminded of Mary and Martha's story found in Luke 10:38-42. Here we find Jesus and his disciples invited into the home of Martha. Like any good host, Martha finds herself working hard to complete the preparations needed. I imagine this may have been the cooking, the cleaning, or the serving. While doing so, Martha approaches Jesus and says, "Lord, don't you care that my sister has left me to do the work by myself? Tell her to help me" (Luke 10:40). We see that Mary was "sitting at the Lord's feet listening to him" (vs. 39).

Jesus responds, "Martha, Martha, you are worried and upset about many things, but few things are needed—or indeed only one. Mary has chosen what is better, and it will not be taken away from her" (vs. 41-42).

Mary chose to pause. She elected to sit at Jesus feet and receive while Martha continued to work tirelessly.

Fellow helper, as you consider how you've spent your time lately, would you say that you have been more like Martha or Mary? In your dedication to caring for those around you, have you taken time to rest and receive or have you continued to work yourself?

Today I remind you that you too need time to pause and receive. You need time to take the helper hat off. Time to rest and reset, just as Jesus did in Mark 1:35.

<u>Read:</u>

Mark 1:35

<u>Reflect:</u>

What might taking the "helper hat" off, look like for me?

| 66 |
"No"

Imagine rushing to work one morning, you stop for your coffee and grab all your things but then *bamm*! There goes your coffee, splattered all over the ground.

This happened to me one morning. I had stopped at Dunkin to get some donut holes and my favorite frozen coffee. When I got to my destination I was scrambling to grab all my things out the car and the coffee slipped from my hands. I hadn't even taken a sip yet. That's a great way to start the morning right?

I had my mind set on that coffee and eventually I got over it but it taught me a valuable lesson - I was trying to carry too much.

What I have learned in my time in this profession thus far, is that I can't carry to much. I can't do it all. I can't say yes to everything. I won't always be able to make space and reschedule appointments. I can't be involved in so many activities after work. I may have to exercise my "no" a little more frequently.

I am reminded of a conversation between Moses and his father-in-law, Jethro in the Old Testament. After God had brought the Israelites out of Egypt, Jethro came to visit Moses. While there, he recognizes all that Moses was doing for the people. He states, "What is this you're doing for the people? Why are you alone sitting as judge, while all the people stand around you from morning until evening? (Exodus 18:14). He continues, ""*What you're doing is not good,*" "*you will certainly wear out both yourself and these people who are with you, because the task is too heavy for you. You can't do it alone"* (vs. 17-18).

Jethro recognized that Moses was carrying to much and he encouraged him to implement a system that would lighten the load. In other words he was telling him, he couldn't do it all.

We can take this same advice. As helpers, yes, we want to help, however at what expense? Today, consider your load. Are there things to delegate? Boundaries that need to be set? Is it time to exercise your "no?"

Prayer:

God I thank you for the care and the compassion that you have placed within me. I thank you that you have given me a desire to help others. Father, I just ask that you would help me to steward this gift well. I recognize that this may mean saying "no" or taking breaks and I'm not so good at that at times, but I acknowledge that I can't do it all. I need you. Amen.

| 67 |

Thank you Lord

As I was driving one day and listening to The Color Purple soundtrack, tears began to fill my eyes. I began to think about how Shug Averie, a well known singer in the movie, had entered Celie's life and it was forever changed. I began to feel gratitude in that moment thinking about how a person can enter your life and it can change forever.

Whether its mentors, friends, family, or other relationships, people have come into my life and incited change that I never imagined. People who have been integral in my walk with the Lord. People who helped me navigate the darkest nights. I imagine you may be able to say the same.

Fellow helper, do you know that you may also be that person for someone? Maybe even a client? *Isn't that kind of amazing?*

I recall clients who have thanked me for helping them at the conclusion of our work together. There have also been clients who emailed years later just to tell me thank you and that they were doing alright. Sometimes it's rare to know how you have truly impacted a client's life but when they do tell you, it fills you with gratitude.

I thank God that He uses us in that way. I thank God that He sees fit to align our paths with someone else's to walk with them through difficult times. It is both a privilege and honor. Psalm 91:1 says, *"I will give thanks to you, LORD, with all my heart; I will tell of all your wonderful deeds."*

Take a few moments to thank God today. Thank Him for showing up in your life fellow helper. Thank Him for those He has placed or will place in your path. Thank Him for the part that you get to play in your clients lives. Thank Him for the way He wants to use you. Express your gratitude to Him today for the wonderful things He has done. Thank you Lord!

<u>Reflect:</u>

What I am I thankful for today?

| 68 |

"Yikes"

As I was writing this, the only word that came to mind was "yikes." So let's unpack it.

Fellow helper, there are some clients who are hard to work with. It's a truth that we all might come face to face with at some point or another.

For a long time I wrestled with this because it felt wrong to admit. It has felt bad to admit that I do not wish to work with particular clients. And it isn't that the clients have done anything "wrong" necessarily, but certain things about their concerns or how they present, may make it a challenge to work with them.

If a fellow helper told me something like this, I'd probably respond with a "yikes" because I get it.

Depending on the setting you may work in, you may not have the option or possibility to refer a client to a different provider or clinician. You may be required to work with that client. So how do you approach it in a way that isn't harmful to that client?

I can recall the very first time I had to navigate this with a client and I would often end session feeling upset and irritated. But eventually I began to pray specific prayers about this.

So if you find yourself in this situation, my first encouragement to you is to take it to God. Philippians 4:6 encourages us to present our requests to God in every situation. Not just particular situations, all situations.

The second thing I had to do is to remember that each client was created in God's image and is loved by Him. John 3:16 says, "For God so loved the world that he gave his one and only Son, that whoever believes in him shall not perish but have eternal life." Replace the [world] with your client's name. For God so loved [client] that He gave...

When we view our client in this lens, reminding ourselves that they too are made in God's image, it changes how we perceive them. I also recognize that it helps me as I sit with them. Rather than feeling "blocked" by my own frustration, I am able to show love and compassion and it becomes easier to sit with them. So yes it's a "yikes" but let's take those "yikes" to God.

Reflect:
Are there any clients that I have difficulty working with?
What is it that may bother me about this client(s)?
What steps can I take to ensure that my feelings are not impeding their progress?

Prayer:
God, today I thank you for [client]. Lord, I admit that I sometimes struggle to sit with them but today I ask that you would help me to view them in a new light. When I meet with them, would you help me to view them as your child, dearly loved and created by you. It's in your name I pray, Amen.

| 69 |

Audacious Prayers

How specific do you get in your prayers to God? I know this is an odd question to ask, but think about it for a second. When you bring concerns to God, do you get specific?

One day a friend of mine shared that as she was traveling she wasn't feeling the best and just wanted to get back home to rest. She shared that on her way to the train she asked God to give her a good seat with leg room. She didn't want to be cramped on the train. When she arrived, the train was moving. She had missed her train. What happened next is what really encouraged me.

Not only did my friend get to board the next train, she didn't have to pay for another ticket, and she was placed in business class. She said that she had a seat to herself, a lot of leg room, and a great view.

God exceeded my friends prayer request. She got specific with her request and God answered.

Audacious prayers are bold prayers. The are specific. I sometimes forget to get specific in my prayers with God. It's not something we have to do (because God already knows) but how cool is it to see a prayer answered exactly in the way that we asked God?

We can ask God to bring 10 new private practice clients. We can ask God to heal the pain that our client is experiencing in their left leg. We can ask God for a cancellation. We can ask God to give us relief from the migraine. We can ask, and if it is in accordance with His plan, watch Him move.

The Bible tells us to "ask and we will receive, seek and we will find, knock and the door will be opened" (Matthew 7:7).

Reflect:

Have I prayed audacious prayers?
What are my current prayer requests?

Prayer:

God I thank you that I get to come to you with big prayers. With bold, audacious prayers. Father thank you that you listen and when my requests align with your will, you answer. Today I bring to you my requests. I ask that: [Speak your requests] It's in your name I pray. Amen.

| 70 |

Truth

When Jesus was in the wilderness Satan tried to tempt Him.

Read: Matthew 4:1-11

How was it that Jesus combated Satan? What did he do to make the devil leave?

Jesus quoted Truth to the devil. He spoke the Word of God. He recited scripture to the devil and he had no choice but to flee.

When we hide God's Word in our hearts, we have the ability to do the same.

One morning, I had just woken up from a dream that was frustrating and I felt discouraged. I remember laying there, still half sleep, and I just began speaking God's Word over myself. I began rehearsing truth from the Bible and who God says I am.

Fellow helper, God says that we are his masterpiece (Ephesians 2:10). We are adopted (Ephesians 1:5). We are light (Matthew 5:14). We are loved (John 3:16). We are chosen (1 Peter 2:9). We are free (John 8:36).

Whether it be after a discouraging dream, in the middle of a session, after a session, during a speaking engagement, or some other experience, we have access to Truth that can combat the lies we are hearing. We don't have to let them consume us.

<u>Read:</u>

Psalm 1:1 -2

Joshua 1:8

<u>Prayer:</u>

God I thank you that I have consistent access to your Word. I thank you that you say that I am loved, chosen, adopted, and so much more. Today I ask that you would allow your Word to wash over me. May I believe wholeheartedly what you say about me. May your Truth be louder than the lies. May your Truth encourage me and empower me to do the work you have for me today. It's in your name I pray, Amen.

Prayer

Lord, today I just want to say thank you. I want to take time to simply express my gratitude for what you've done in my life and continue to do.

Lord I thank you for the work that you have called me to do and the ways that you have used me thus far.

Lord You have equipped me for this work and I do not take it for granted. In Exodus 31, I learn that you equipped Oholiab and Bezalel with the skills and abilities needed to build your Holy Tabernacle, the place where you would dwell with your people, and I thank you for also equipping me with the skills and abilities needed to care for the hearts and souls of those around me. Those I meet with for counseling.

Lord I am thankful to be used by you. I am thankful to be deemed worthy of such a calling as this. Lord would you continue to lead me and guide me. Speak to me and speak through me Lord. I surrender this gift to you and ask that you would always get the glory. Thank you Lord. Thank you today.

It's in your name I pray, amen.

<u>Song for reflection:</u>
Gratitude - Brandon Lake

| 71 |

Questions

These are all the beginning of questions or statements I've heard in sessions. Clients questioning why things have happened to them. Questioning why other people seem to get the things they want. Clients questioning when things will go well for them. Questions that you and I would not have the answers to.

I am reminded of the psalmist in Psalm 73 who also had questions and longed for answers. For several verses he wonders why certain people don't have troubles, live painless lives, and prosper, while he gets "trouble all day long and pain every morning" (vs. 14). He couldn't understand. Was he doing something "wrong?" Did he deserve it? Why?

How might you respond to a client sitting across from you pleading for answers? Longing to understand? How do you sit with uncertainty in your life? What truth do you cling onto when you don't understand?

Fellow helper, we will not always have the answers nor the words to answer these 'why' questions. We must accept that truth. However, I have found a few things helpful in these moments: 1) empathizing with my clients and letting them know I too wish they had the answers they are longing for, 2) sometimes I share that I believe things can/will get better, 3) I remind myself that their pain has a purpose and how God uses our suffering, and 4) in cases that a client is a believer, I might explore with them how God uses our pain.

There is no "right" way to approach these questions, but I think sometimes our clients just need to know that it is normal to wrestle with "why" questions and that even we have longed/long for answers.

At the end of the day, we won't always know why things happen fellow helper, but as believers in Jesus Christ, we can rest knowing the things we experience and what our clients experience is never in vain. God has a plan.

Read:

1 Peter 5:10

2 Corinthians 4:17

Reflect:

How might I approach these moments with clients?

What do I believe or know to be true about suffering?

| 72 |
Provider

When I think about God as a provider, the story of Elijah the prophet, a widow, and her son comes to mind. This can be found in 1 Kings 17.

As the story unfolds we see that there is a drought in the land of Zarephath and God sends Elijah to this widow who will supply him food. As Elijah meets with the widow she basically tells him that she has no food and she was preparing a final meal for herself and her son for them to die. Elijah tells the woman to make a loaf of bread and then shares a word with her from the Lord: "the jar of flour will not be used up and the jug of oil will not run dry until the day the Lord sends rain on the land (vs. 14). The next verse says, "she went away and did as Elijah had told her. So there was food every day for Elijah and for the woman and for her family" (vs. 15).

This woman was prepared to die! She was preparing for her final meal, yet God stepped in at the right time and provided for her.

Today, if you find yourself wondering if God will provide, I encourage you to take time reflecting on the full passage of 1 Kings 17 fellow helper.

What God did for this woman, we can trust that He will do for us, for our clients, and our families too.

<u>Read:</u>

Luke 12:24

Prayer:

Father thank you that you are a provider. You Word says in Philippians 4:19, that every need you will supply. Lord, would you help me today to trust you as provider for me, for my family, for my clients. When all seems lost and hopeless, you will come through. You will provide. Thank you Father. Amen.

| **73** |

"Do not pass me by"

There's an old hymn that goes,

"Pass me not, O gentle Savior,

Hear my humble cry;

While on others Thou art calling,

Do not pass me by.

Savior, Savior,

Hear my humble cry;

While on others Thou art calling,

Do not pass me by."

One day as I was washing dishes this song came on and I couldn't help but listen more intently to the words. "Do not pass me by" kept sticking out to me. I'm pretty sure it brought me to tears.

I can recall times in my life where I've felt that God "passed me by." Like God just didn't see me or hear me. This person got their blessing, received their healing, got this or that, but I haven't. I question, "God did I do something wrong? Did I miss you?" I felt overlooked, forgotten, passed by.

What I am reminded today is that God is not a God who passes us by. He never has and He never will. The Bible shows us countless testimonies of men and women who were cared for when they were forgotten by others. This included women, Samaritans, lepers, demon possessed, sickly, etc. These were people who were deemed to be "outcasts" in their day. God did not pass them by. Jesus saw them.

In the same way, God does not pass us by. He doesn't pass our family by. He doesn't pass our clients by. Sometimes it may feel like it or seem like it, when prayers go unanswered or longings unfulfilled, however we can trust that He hears us, sees us, and will not pass us by.

Consider these verses:

- Psalm 34:15, "The eyes of the Lord are on the righteous, and his ears are attentive to their cry."
- Psalm 34:17, "The righteous cry out, and the LORD hears them; he delivers them from all their troubles."
- Psalm 18:6, "In my distress I called to the Lord; I cried to my God for help. From his temple he heard my voice; my cry came before him, into his ears."
- Psalm 116:1, "I love the Lord, for he heard my voice; he heard my cry for mercy."
- Psalm 40:1, "I waited patiently for the Lord; He turned to me and heard my cry. He lifted me out of the slimy pit, out of the mud and mire; He set my feet on a rock and gave me a firm place to stand."

Today, be reminded of the truth that God does not pass us by. Hold it close to your heart. Ponder it. Reflect on it.

Truth for today:

God hears my cry. He will never pass me by.

| 74 |

The things I love

"This is what I have observed to be good: that it is appropriate for a person to eat, to drink and to find satisfaction in their toilsome labor under the sun during the few days of life God has given them—for this is their lot. Moreover, when God gives someone wealth and possessions, and the ability to enjoy them, to accept their lot and be happy in their toil—this is a gift of God." - Ephesians 5:18-19

When was the last time that you did something you truly enjoyed? The things that make you feel good? The things that are like a breathe of fresh air? The things that make you feel warm and fuzzy inside? Content?

One day as I was leaving church, I decided to go treat myself to a frozen coffee, one of my favorites. It was about January at this time but the weather wasn't unbearably cold or anything. As I drove there I also cracked my window a little to let some of the crisp air in. The thought crossed my mind, "I want to do more of the things I love this year."

In the midst of caring for others we sometimes forget to do the things we love. We forget to care for ourselves. We forget to treat ourselves. We, sometimes unintentionally, place ourselves on the back burner.

But what I have recognized is that when I take time for myself, I feel more inclined, more prepared, more energized to help others.

Consider this quote from Author Eleanor Brown: "Rest and self-care are important. When you take time to replenish your spirit, it allows you to serve from the overflow. You cannot serve from an empty vessel."

To replenish is to fill something up again, to recharge, to restock something. Doing more of what you love replenishes your supply, fellow helper. It gives you new energy and drive not only to counsel and work with those in your care, but also those in your life. So I encourage you, I plead with you, to do more of the things you love fellow helper. You work so hard every day. Please also give yourself time to enjoy your favorite things.

- *From: A fellow helper who also needs to to do more of the things she loves*

75

Moving forward

I need to be honest about something. Growing up, I use to hate seeing parents have their kids wearing those leash backpacks. It resembled a leash for dogs only it was connected to a backpack. I didn't understand the purpose of them. I always felt that they were restricting the kids from freedom to explore. But I guess that was the purpose haha. They were used to protect them from danger. They were a safeguard to keep the kids from running off.

As I think about Paul's letter to the church of Ephesus, I can see how he also wanted to protect the believers from danger. He wasn't trying to control them, he wanted to safeguard them. Paul urged them to *"get rid of all bitterness, rage and anger, brawling and slander, along with every form of malice,"* (Ephesians 4:31). Paul knew the danger of running around freely, holding on to these things. He tells us just verses earlier that anger *"gives a foothold to the devil"* (vs. 27).

There are disastrous effects of holding on to anger. Rumination, reliving negative experiences, unpleasant emotions, resentment. Anger keeps us stuck in a never-ending loop. It limits us from walking in the true freedom given to us by Christ. It hurts us. Not only this, but as clinician's we know the effects that some of these things can have on mental health.

I'm sure you've worked with clients who have been holding on to anger in their hearts. Anger at their abusers, anger at their families, their partners, the list could go on.

Likewise, I'm sure you've experienced anger and bitterness towards someone in your life.

As you sit with your clients today, consider if anger may be interfering with their progress, fellow helper. How might you help them move through it? Is it hindering them from moving forward in their healing?

Reflect:

Has anger been hindering my growth or progress?
Are there people I need to release and forgive?

Read:

James 1:10
Psalm 37:8

76

Surrendered outcomes

Commit to the LORD whatever you do, and your plans will succeed.
In his heart a man plans his course, but the LORD determines his steps.
- Proverbs 16:3, 9

Have you ever found yourself wanting something to go well so you work overtime to make it happen? To make sure every detail and thing is covered? To make sure it works out perfectly? Maybe you were planning for an initial assessment and the client takes seemingly forever to do the paperwork, cutting down your time to assess? Maybe you were hoping to wrap up things with a family you were working with and some last minute issue arose? Maybe you worked with another provider to help your client access a higher level of care and for some reason it didn't work out?

We live in a world where despite our best efforts to prepare, plan, or predict, things happen that are outside of our control. Things that may disrupt our plans and change the outcomes. I've seen this countless times but what I have learned is that in this work, we must surrender all outcomes. This doesn't mean that we shouldn't consider goals, we can't have hopes, or make a plan, but I am suggesting that we surrender the outcomes of what may happen.

Surrendering outcomes is about letting go of control, the potential for disappointment, and the possibility of frustration. Just think about it, how might you feel after working overtime to make something happen and it doesn't turn out the way you expected? I'd be frustrated. Maybe even annoyed.

Surrendering outcomes is a daily task. When we surrender our hopes, our plans, and our expectations to God, it releases us from overworking ourselves to achieve a certain outcome. It releases us from perfection and control. It releases us from the potential of disappointment.

As you set goals with clients, personal goals for yourself, or professional goals, remember to surrender the outcomes to God...trusting that whatever will be will be. *Que sera sera.*

Reflect:

What areas of my life do I need to surrender outcomes?

What happens when I surrender outcomes?

Read:

Proverbs 3:5-6

| 77 |

Plugged into the Source

"Seek the Lord and his strength; seek his presence continually!"
– 1 Chronicles 16:11

One day God chose to speak to me through a little charging mishap with my phone. My frustration could have easily distracted me from hearing what He wanted to speak, but instead I obliged.

As I was cleaning one day, I realized my phone was about to die so I ran to go plug it in. Once plugged in, I continued to clean up before heading to my next destination. I can't remember exactly where I was headed but as I went to grab my phone I found it at the exact percentage it was when I initially plugged it in. A closer look made me realize that it was plugged in yet not charging at all. A little wiggle of the cord and I felt the quick buzz that indicated that it was now charging.

As I walked away from that moment with my nearly dead phone, God reminded me of the importance of being plugged into the source, aka Him. It's not enough to just log into my Bible app, read a verse and go about my day. That would be the equivalent of plugging in my phone for maybe 1 min. He wants more.

With the busyness of life and all the daily responsibilities, time with God can become scarce. He can be placed on the back burner while everything else comes first.

We forget to plug in and sometimes we are burnt out before we recognize it. Our battery has gone out. It happens to us all.

But the truth is that I am a better clinician when I spend daily time with God. I am a better friend, a better colleague, a better daughter. When we are plugged into the source, in daily conversation and communion with God, He charges us up to do the work He has required of us...

What percent is your battery at fellow helper? Is it time to plug back in to the Source?

The cool thing is that God is always ready and available, excited for some quality time with you.

Reflect:

How am I currently feeling?

Have I spent time with God lately?

Truth for today:

Time with God, equips me to do the work He has required of me.

| 78 |

A glimmer of hope

One day a new client entered my office for an initial assessment. She appeared downcast. She looked down as she walked to the chair she was going to sit in and settled her belongings on the table. She didn't smile and she barely said a word. She was slightly guarded and short with her responses. She stated that she felt alone. She was angry. She was tired of struggling with what felt like a cycle in her life.

That same client walked out of my office with a glimmer of hope. A slight brightness appeared on her face as she walked out the door. I saw a look of relief as if she could breathe again.

It really brings tears to my eyes thinking about the whole encounter because I believe that God used me to bring light to her situation. Hope to a darkness she had been experiencing for months.

When we spend time with God we too, can leave with a glimmer of hope. I recognize that when I surround myself with those who uplift me and encourage me, I leave with a new glimmer of hope. When I leave church on Sundays, I have a glimmer of hope. Seeing a change in others circumstances, gives me a glimmer of hope.

Hope changes things. It gives us the ability to believe for change despite what we may see.

Isaiah 40:31 says, *"But those who wait for the Lord [who expect, look for, and hope in Him] Will gain new strength and renew their power; They will lift up their wings [and rise up close to God] like eagles [rising toward the sun]; They will run and not become weary, They will walk and not grow tired."*

As helpers, I believe that we possess this sincere hope for our clients. We believe their situation will get better. We hope that they will experience the relief they are longing for. We have hope for them, even when they may not possess it themselves. Fellow helper, your hope for your clients is powerful and it shines through you. As you meet with your clients remember that just as your light is contagious, so is your hope.

Read:
Psalm 39:7

Psalm 130:5-6

Truth for today:
My hope is contagious.

Motivated

"Let love and kindness be the motivation behind all that you do." - 1 Corinthians 16:14 TPT

As a helper, a believer...a human, I hold this scripture near to my heart.

As I browsed a home goods store one evening, looking for the perfect picture to complete my living room wall...Bam! I stumbled across this gray and white sign with this scripture beautifully written across it. It resonated with me deeply so I knew I had to get it.

If you are in this field of helping, I imagine that you possess kindness, empathy, you care for people, and you might enjoy helping others. It would hard to do this work without some of those traits. But what I recognize is that love and kindness should always influence and affect our work.

Why you may ask? Because the entire Gospel is about love and kindness. God sending his one and only son to die for us, is the ultimate example of love and kindness. Not only this but In Jesus' time on earth He demonstrated love and kindness, even to those who were considered "lowly" or rejected by society. His love and kindness was available to all.

Jesus teaches us that love and kindness are about showing respect and generosity to everyone we encounter without conditions attached. This love should motivate and influence how we counsel every client in our care.

<u>**Prayer:**</u>

God I thank you for your ultimate example of love and kindness by sending your son to die for me and my sins. I could never thank you enough for the sacrifice you made. Lord, in a world that lacks kindness and love, would you continue to grow and develop it in me. As I sit with my clients, allow this love and kindness radiate through me. May my words, my actions, my interventions be pleasing to you and helpful to those that I sit with. Help me to remember my why - your love and sacrifice. Let love and kindness motivate me daily as I continue to do this work that you have equipped me for. Amen.

| 80 |

Empowered to speak

Speaking is something that we have to do in our field of work every day or every session. Unless you are working with someone who would rather be anywhere else. Then I imagine a lot of silence. When I think about speaking I think about Moses and Aaron in the Old Testament. I think about how Moses, was seemingly mortified and filled with dread at the thought of having to speak on behalf of God to the Israelites. I think of how Moses asked God to just send someone else (Exodus 4).

I have been there. I have been in the place of Moses, filled with burning thoughts, ideas, or encouragement but also filled with dread and fear of opening my mouth. Whether it be to one individual or multiple. Whether I'm in a meeting or the grocery store, there was a time when I felt mute. The words just wouldn't come out.

We can also experience this with our clients. Maybe we are afraid to speak about something they have shared out of fear that we may offend them. Maybe it's fear that we may be wrong. Maybe it's fear that our words may not come out right. Maybe it's imposter syndrome and feeling that we don't really know what we are talking about?

Regardless of where you find yourself, I'd like to share this reminder that God empowers us to speak.

Read: Exodus 4

There are 2 times in this chapter that God says, "I will help you speak and will teach you what to say/do" (vs. 12, 15). Now I probably would have been nervous too if God told me to go speak to Pharoah, the ruler of Egypt at that time. Not only that but Moses would be the leader to God's nation and have to speak to thousands of people. That's a big job. Nonetheless, God had a purpose and a plan.

God empowered Moses, He empowered Aaron, and He can empower us as well.

Truth for today:

God empowers me to speak.

Read:

Jeremiah 1:9

Matthew 10:19-20

Prayer

Lord, I just want to thank you for my clients. Lord, I care deeply for them and I know that is only because of your immense love for them working through me. God I pray that they would know that they are cared for, they are loved, and they are worthy.

As I begin to picture each client who I've crossed paths with, I thank you for their quirks, for their unique personality, and how you have designed them. Lord, I pray that in their time in therapy they would grow to see themselves in the way that you do. May they know that they are deserving of healthy, loving relationships. May they know that their past does not define them. May they know that their experiences have a greater purpose that they can see. May they embrace who they are and see the ways that they stand out from the rest. May they celebrate their individuality and not get caught in comparison. May they receive the relief and support they are longing for.

Lord I thank you that I play a small part in their journey. I thank you that I get to sit with them and cry, laugh, challenge, support, encourage, and assist them in their time of need. They are precious in your sight. They are worthy of your love and care.

Lord I surrender each client to you. Would you speak to me and lead me as I meet with them. Would you help me to ask the questions that need to be asked. Would help me to be fully present and attentive. Would you allow them to experience a safe and healing space.

I know that I don't know it all and nor see the full picture of their lives but you do and I thank you that you have equipped me to work with them. Thank you that you have orchestrated our paths to cross. I trust you Father. I lean on you and seek your guidance today. Thank you for using me. Thank you for my clients. It's in your name I pray, Amen.

| 81 |

Lay it down

Confession: I'm a therapist and sometimes I worry about work.

Have you ever caught yourself thinking about conversations you need to have with clients? Moments you wonder how a client is doing? Worry if a client will be okay? Think about your schedule for the next day?

One day I caught myself thinking about many of these things. I had been home for work for an hour or so, yet my mind was still at work. I was completely absent minded from what I was actually doing. Once I snapped back into the present, I took a deep breath and was able to put work aside. I couldn't continue to allow worry to consume my evening. It was exhausting. In that moment I felt God gently remind me that I was worried about many things that I needed to give to Him.

The Bible often urges us to "cast our cares," "keep our minds stayed on Him," "do not worry," and more. Consider Philippians 4:6-7 which says, *"Don't worry about anything; instead, pray about everything. Tell God what you need, and thank him for all he has done. Then you will experience God's peace, which exceeds anything we can understand. His peace will guard your hearts and minds as you live in Christ Jesus"* (Philippians 4:6-7 NLT).

In other words, peace follows the action of giving something to God.

If you find that you sometimes struggle to leave work at work, I encourage you to lay it down fellow helper. Make it a daily practice to visualize yourself giving each client, each worry, or each concern to God. Close your eyes, take a deep breath, and lay it down.

Read:

Isaiah 26:3

Reflect:

Do I struggle to leave work at work?
What do I find myself worrying about?

| 82 |

Listen

"Listen to my instruction and be wise; do not disregard it."
- Proverbs 8:32

As people who practice and specialize in the skill of listening, we can be terrible at listening to ourselves at times. It's kind of like that saying "doctors are the worst patients." It's so true.

This makes me think about a recent experience that I had. For months I was sick on and off. I had headaches and nausea, some days my throat would hurt, other days it was aches, fatigue, or pains. I initially attributed it to traveling during that time however as it continued over time, I realized that maybe it was something more. Maybe God was trying to tell me something.

I wasn't listening to Him. Here I was pushing through work, pushing through worship at church, pushing through what I was experiencing, while God was urging me to stop. I was anxious and stressed about a decision I had to make but it was presenting in a physical form and I wasn't paying attention.

Sometimes this can happen as we show up daily for our clients. As we present to work. As we go about our day to day routines. I think this is why body scans are found to be so useful - taking time to intentionally scan our bodies for any tension or stress.

As we all know, when anxious and stressed, our thoughts can be a jumbled mess and racing. In my case, God needed my attention and He needed me to slow down, hence the physical symptoms. In those few months, He was trying to give instruction while I was so busy trying to push through and figure it out myself.

Fellow helper, I'm a firm believer that God will get our attention by any means necessary when He needs us to do something. Consider the story of Balaam the sorcerer. God "opened the donkey's mouth" and it spoke to Balaam.

Read: Numbers 22:21-29

While I don't believe that God would speak to us through a donkey today (*though He could if He wanted to*), I think that He can and will use anything.

So my encouragement to you is to practice listening. Practice listening to your body and listening to God. Are there ways He has been trying to speak to you lately? Have you been listening?

Prayer:

God I thank you that you love us so much that you will stop at nothing to get our attention. Lord help me to be more attentive to myself and to moments when you could be speaking. Open my eyes that I may see, my heart that I may receive, my ears that I may listen, and my mind that I may understand.

It's in your name I pray. Amen.

| 83 |

Do not covet

For a long time I thought the quote "comparison is the thief of joy" was from scripture. I mean it sounds like something you would find in the Bible. However, while it's not from the Bible I think it's important to highlight that comparison can lead to what the Bible often refers to "coveting." Coveting is essentially wanting what someone else has. It's deemed a sin.

When God gave Moses the 10 commandments, He included coveting. Exodus 20:17 says, *"You must not covet your neighbor's house. You must not covet your neighbor's wife, male or female servant, ox or donkey, or anything else that belongs to your neighbor."*

The Bible actually has a lot to say about coveting, including that it *"defiles or corrupts us"* (Mark 7:20-22 ESV).

When we compare we often feel discontent and in that discontentment we can begin to covet, having a strong desire for what someone else has.

We start to compare our lives, our success, our abilities, our bodies, our spouses, the list could go on and on. I think we all do it at one point or another in our lives.

For awhile I would compare myself as a clinician. Comparing my knowledge, my abilities, my clinical skills to my colleagues and it was not helpful at all.

Would you agree that comparing your life has not been effective? What about wanting what others around you have?

The truth is we can always find things that we wished were different or better in our lives, but fellow helper we must be mindful of comparison and coveting in our lives and in our profession. Maybe that's by practicing gratitude. Maybe it's by seeking God and having an honest conversation about what you feel is lacking. Maybe it's by taking a break from social media. But God is clear that we should not covet.

<u>Reflect:</u>

How do I manage tendencies to compare myself to others?
Are there things that I may be coveting currently?

His Word is good

In 2023, I fell in love with a song titled "He always provides" by One House and Chandler Moore. It made it to my daily Spotify playlist and of course it ended up on my 2023 Wrapped that Spotify shares with it's users at the end of every year.

A particular portion of this song states, "Cause He says what He means, there's nothing in between. In my heart I believe, every word that He speaks. Oh, Lord, your Word is good to me."

The first thing that comes to my mind when I hear this part of the song is that God is a man of His word. He can be trusted. However, I'd be remiss not to acknowledge the fact that in seasons of waiting it can be hard to believe that God says what He means. Can anyone else agree?

Maybe we felt God speak something about our lives, our situations, our business, and it has yet to come to pass. *Did I hear Him wrong? Did He really say that? Maybe He meant something else? Will He really do it?* We begin to question ourselves and we begin to question God. I have been there and I imagine that you have as well fellow helper.

Today, if you find yourself in a season of waiting for God's promise to come to pass, I encourage you to hold on to the truth given to us in this song. What God speaks to you, He absolutely means. The Bible is clear that God is not a man that He should lie. Numbers 23:19 says it this way, *"God is not human, that he should lie, not a human being, that he should change his mind. Does he speak and then not act? Does he promise and not fulfill?"*

While His timing may not always meet our preferred expectation, we can trust that He is good on His Word to us fellow helper.

In moments of doubt, cling to the words of this song and hold Numbers 23:19 close to your heart.

Prayer:

God I thank you that you are a man of your Word. I thank you that you do not and will not lie. Help me believe that your Word is good. Help me to trust it and believe it in my heart even when I can't see or I begin to doubt. Thank you Father. It's in your name I pray. Amen.

Truth for today:

God's Word is good.

| 85 |

Feelings

When I began graduate school, I questioned if I could even be in this field. It wasn't necessarily because I was doubting myself, though that was a small piece of it. It was because I was always called "too emotional." Whether it was by my peers or my own perception, I knew that I felt deeply. It could be a movie, it could be a song, it could be in casual conversation...the tears always came. Maybe they were happy tears, sometimes they were sad tears, but tears nonetheless. I believed that I couldn't do this job because I was too emotional.

I recall the first time I cried with a client. Initially, I tried to hold back but the weight and pain of what my client was sharing hit me. I hated what they had to experience. I could vicariously feel that my client was hurting.

What I have learned is that it is okay to have an emotional response to what some clients are sharing. I do not make the moment about me, but I do lean in and hear my client in a deeper way.

There may be times where you may have an emotional response to what a client is sharing. Maybe you hold back the tears? Maybe you believe you have to remain neutral? Maybe you let the tears fall? How you decide to respond is up to you fellow helper, but it is not "bad" nor is it "wrong" to experience emotion during sessions. It does not mean you are weak or less effective. It does not undermine your skill. It does not make the session about you. In many cases it will not interfere or damage the relationship. You are a human that experiences emotion just like any other person sitting across from you.

Romans 12:15 tells us to *"rejoice with those who rejoice, weep with those who weep."* Similarly, Ecclesiates 3:1 tells us, *"there is a time for everything, and a season for every activity under the heavens: a time to weep and a time to laugh, a time to mourn and a time to dance (vs.4)."*

Fellow helper, you may hear heartbreaking stories that bring tears but also know that God designed you with emotion, to be felt.

So from one fellow helper to another, it's okay to show your humanness. It's okay to feel. And even Jesus found himself deeply moved and He himself wept when His friend Lazarus died.

<u>Read:</u>
John 11
(Emphasis on vs. 32-35)

| 86 |

Ask God

"If you need wisdom, ask our generous God, and he will give it to you. He will not rebuke you for asking."
- James 1:5 NLT

One of the wisest things a person can do is to ask for help when they are faced with a situation that they are uncertain about. However, as we all know, asking for help can be difficult to do. Maybe it's uncomfortable. Maybe you feel like you shouldn't need to ask for help. Maybe you feel like asking for help makes you a burden. Maybe it's pride. Maybe it's fearing judgment. Maybe you believe that you will receive inadequate advice. Maybe it's something else.

When it comes to clients, asking God for help is one of the best pieces of advice I can offer you fellow helper. You will be met with situations, presentations, and circumstances that you will feel unprepared or uncertain about. It's not a matter of if, but when.

I can recall times sitting in session and silently pleading with God to help me with a client. For Him to give me the wisdom and the Words to say in moments I had nothing. I had no words, no supportive reflection, no questions...just my presence, my empathy, and my mmms. And while sometimes that may be enough, I knew it would not suffice for every session. I needed wisdom, I needed guidance. I needed God to intervene.

James 1:5 reminds us that when we ask for wisdom, God will give it to us. He isn't rude. He doesn't treat us as if we should know the answer. He is generous and provides his loving direction.

I am constantly reminded of my need for God in life but also working in this profession. I simply cannot afford to do this work without Him involved. I do not believe that I can help any client without Gods wisdom and guidance. Because who knows my clients better than the Creator?

As the scripture says, God will not rebuke us for asking. In fact I think He delights in the fact that we do ask and acknowledge that we can't do it apart from Him.

Read:

Mark 11:24

1 John 5:14-15

Truth for today:

When I need direction, I can ask God.

Sometimes

Sometimes you will get discouraged in session, between sessions, or after sessions. Sometimes clients will drop out of therapy. Sometimes clients won't like working with you. Sometimes things happen that disappoint us. Sometimes we may feel rejected because of these things.

How do you navigate the disappointment that may come with some of these experiences? What messages do you tell yourself fellow helper?

Maybe you had a client and you felt that you all had a good rapport developing but they suddenly drop off. The disappear. This happened to me once and I wrestled with it for awhile because I wondered what happened. I was confused.

I'm sure we can all agree that we would love it if we could help every client that we come across but sometimes that won't be the case.

When these 'sometimes' moments come, *because they will*, I find that I have to pause and sit with the confusion or disappointment I might feel. Many times that looks like closing my office door, sitting against the wall, and breathing. I have to remind myself that it is okay when these things happen. It's okay if a client doesn't want to work with me. It's okay if a client drops off and I don't know why. It's okay if I feel lost with a client. It might hurt but it really is okay.

Proverbs 19:21 says, *"Many are the plans in a person's heart, but it is the Lord's purpose that prevails."* Likewise, Isaiah 14:24 says, *"The Lord Almighty has sworn, "Surely, as I have planned, so it will be, and as I have purposed, so it will happen."*

It could be that we had one thing in mind, but God had another and His plan will always prevail. That has to be okay.

We may not be the best fit for a client, their family, or their unique needs. A client may disappear on us for reasons unknown to us. But that also has to be okay. These things don't always feel good, but we must sit with it, acknowledge it, and then we must let it go for our own peace of mind.

Sometimes things will happen and that has to be okay.

Reflect:

Are there experiences that did not go as expected that I need to let go of?

How do I feel knowing that I won't have all the answers or connect with every client?

Prayer:

God you know more than anyone what rejection feels like. Your Word tells us that we do not have a high priest who is unable to empathize with our weaknesses, but we have one who has been tempted in every way. Lord It's not the best feeling in the world when a client doesn't want to work with me or drops out or progress isn't made, but God I surrender every feeling to you right now. I choose to let go. I choose to believe that when I don't understand what may have happened, you had a plan. Thank you Lord. It's in your name I pray. Amen.

| 88 |

Loved completely

Fellow helper you are loved completely. Its not because you've helped/will help countless people, but because God loves you immensely. He gave his one and only son because He loved you (John 3:16).

God's love for us isn't conditional. It isn't measurable. He doesn't divvy out His love based on who has helped the most people, who has the most clients, how many "success" stories we have, or how we feel about ourselves. God's love is absolute.

I've had days where it feels like all of my clients are going downhill. I've also had days where I feel like I'm going downhill myself. What I've had to remind myself in these moments is that my worth as a clinician does not diminish on "bad days." My worth as a clinician doesn't change if my client's symptoms worsen. My worth as a clinician doesn't decrease if I am struggling. I am still valuable and still loved.

Our measuring stick for our worth and value must be found in Jesus not in the outcomes of therapy or how we feel about ourselves fellow helper. Scripture constantly tells us of our worth in Jesus Christ.

<u>Read:</u>
Matthew 10:31
Romans 5:8
Luke 12:6-7

So today, know that you are loved and valuable even when you are:

Struggling	*Unfocused*
Burnt out	*Experiencing compassion*
Depressed	*fatigue*
Thriving	*Happy*
Overwhelmed	*Feeling ineffective*
Can't fill your caseload	*Lost*
Uncertain	*Feeling like a failure*

From one fellow helper to another, I hope you stand on truth today that you are, will, and always will be loved completely.

| 89 |

Limitless

God is limitless. I am reminded of this truth every time I sit at the beach and stare at the seemingly endless body of water.

Sarah and Abraham didn't believe that they would get pregnant in their old age and fulfill God's promise to them (Genesis 17). God had promised them that many descendants would come from them, however time passed and Sarah and Abraham still did not have a son. Finally, Genesis 21 opens, *"The Lord kept his word and did for Sarah exactly what he had promised. She became pregnant, and she gave birth to a son for Abraham in his old age. This happened at just the time God had said it would"* (vs. 1-2).

Abraham and Sarah's story reminds me of just how limitless God is. In their old age, their son Isaac was born.

When it seemed impossible because of their age, God made it happen. He is not confined to the same limits and constraints that we have. He can make the impossible possible. He can make a way out of no way. He can do anything.

When I think about my clients, I stand amazed just thinking about how God can show up and move in their lives. I may have one approach or thing in mind for their healing, but who knows what God has in mind. I cannot even imagine or fathom what He can do.

Truth is, it is hard to imagine all that God can do. 1 Corinthians 2:9 says, *"But it is just as the Scriptures say, "What*

God has planned for people who love him is more than eyes have seen or ears have heard. It has never even entered our minds!" (CEV).

As I mentioned before, there are times where I may consider an approach or way to help my clients, however, I continue to recognize that God ultimately knows the things that He will accomplish and how He will do it in my clients life. This should excite us.

I think about a client of mine who I've exhausted all options, treatment suggestions, and resources. I know that our time in therapy allows them to feel seen and heard, however this client has several ongoing physical concerns that continue to interfere with functioning and mood. Though it can be difficult to see my client suffer, I am also excited as I think about the ways that God will bring healing or relief. I may not know when or how but I believe that He will. Because while we may have limits to what we can do, our God is limitless fellow helper.

| 90 |

Believe for them

Some clients come to us in a season of suffering, crisis, and distress.

As a believer, we have the choice to hold onto our hope in Jesus Christ in the middle of our distress. Our hope in Christ can give us an ounce of strength to keep going. In Jesus, we know that our suffering is not in vain nor wasted. That doesn't make it enjoyable, but we know that there is a purpose for it that will later be revealed.

So many times we sit across from clients who are suffering in the present or have experienced suffering in their past. Many times their suffering has transformed their view of people, negatively impacted their view of life, and left them wondering "if there is a God, why would He allow this to happen."

For the clients who have openly identified as Christian and indicated they would like to discuss faith in sessions, this is a conversation I welcome and look forward to having. But I have also worked with clients who don't identify as believers. In those situations, I find myself pausing to consider how I may instill hope.

Sometimes this may look like finding exceptions when the client didn't feel as though they were suffering. Sometimes it looks like inviting them to explore what changes they would like to see and empowering them in their decision making. Sometimes I offer my own hope. My own hope that their situation can get better and they have the ability to bounce back from it.

Whether a client is a believer or not, I hold on to hope, acknowledging in my heart that nothing my client experiences will be wasted and that it has a purpose greater than either of us may understand.

As you work with clients now and in the future, remember that your hope alone can play a significant part in the therapy process. When your clients find it hard to believe, believe for them fellow helper.

Prayer:

God I thank you that in seasons of calamity, crisis, and suffering, your hope anchors my soul. God I pray that this hope may exude through me for the client that believes and for the client that may not believe it you. Father help me instill hope in my clients as they navigate various circumstances. Help them to believe things can get better, and when they can't, help me to believe for them. It's In your name I pray. Amen.

Prayer

Lord, thank you that you are the source of wisdom and direction. Thank you that when I feel lost and don't know where to go, you are there. Thank you for your love. Thank you for your comfort. Thank you that you guide me.

Lord today I ask for clarity and direction. Father sometimes I feel like I am in a season of complete uncertainty. I feel like I've reached a dead end or a block in the road. I am desperate for direction and I am struggling to hear your voice. Father, speak to me. Help me to know that you are not too far from my reach. Help me remember that you give me wisdom and direction. You light my path and order my steps. Father just as you led the Israelites through the wilderness, help me to trust that you will lead me.

May my ears be pressed to your lips so that your voice is certain and clear? God I don't want to question or wonder if it is you speaking. Increase my ability to hear you Father.

Lord you are so good. You are so kind, so loving, so patient, and so faithful. Thank you that you hear my prayer. Thank you in advance for what you will do. Amen.

| 91 |

To be liked

Early on as a resident in counseling, I would constantly get anxiety when working with clients. I wondered if it would be a good fit, how the initial assessment would go, if they would keep coming. The thoughts could go on. The bottomline: I wanted them to like me as a clinician.

My supervisor caught on to this quick however I was in denial. She would ask if I was "afraid" to ask my client certain questions or point out certain behaviors. For a while, I reasoned, no I'm not afraid, I just didn't know how to go there. Eventually I had to acknowledge the fact that I really was afraid to "go there." I was afraid that I might offend or upset a client. Afraid that they wouldn't like me.

It was a deeper concern that I had to work through personally and in supervision in order to effectively work with my clients, but once I addressed that fear and anxiety, the skill of challenging became my best friend. I gently confronted and challenged my clients without fear of being disliked or upsetting them. Not only this but as I grew more comfortable in my identity in Christ, my role as a therapist, and in my position that fear decreased. I would be remiss to think that I am alone.

Sure we all may have an underlying desire to be liked, however at what cost? If you find yourself constantly refraining from saying certain things that may ultimately benefit the client, tiptoeing around concerns, hesitating to point out patterns or behaviors, I'd encourage you to explore where that hesitation is stemming from. Whether you are seasoned, new to the field, fresh out of graduate school, or considering this profession, it's important to shine a light on this fear because we may do a great disservice to our clients by trying to be "liked."

<u>Helpful reminders:</u>

You can gently confront and challenge clients.
You are their therapist and are there to help them grow, not a friend who might "sugar coat" things.

Jesus loved all people AND if we look at the Gospels (Matthew, Mark, Luke, and John) we see that He did not shy away from correcting, challenging, or helping people understand deeper issues. He did it with love, tact, and directness. We can do the same fellow helper.

| 92 |

I see you

"But as for you, brothers and sisters, do not grow weary in doing good."
- 2 Thessalonians 3:13

People rarely talk about the countless hours that go into this field. The CEU's you need, the graduate school, the papers, the internship, the license renewals, time spent preparing for sessions, time in sessions, studying for licensure exams, the list could go on and on. It can become tiring. Exhausting. You may have families you are caring for, another job, and other responsibilities that leave you questioning when you will get that next break. Fellow helper, I get that and I see you.

If you are starting graduate school, I see you.
If you are in your practicum/internship, I see you.
If you are preparing to begin your residency, I see you.
If you are on the brink of licensure, I see you.
Studying for your licensure exam, I see you.
Licensed and trying to keep up with your CEU's, I see you.
Starting your private practice, I see you.

Galatians 6:9 says, *"Let's not get tired of doing good, because in time we'll have a harvest if we don't give up (CEB)."*

The work that you continue to do and the hours that you invest, are not wasted. You will get to see and experience a reward from your work. Remember to rest when necessary. Listen to your body. Pace yourself. Treat yourself. And I pray that a break is on it's way to you fellow helper.

<u>Read:</u>

1 Corinthians 15:58

Hebrews 10:35-36

| 93 |

The other side

The book of Job takes us you on an emotional rollercoaster. We meet a man who seemingly has it all. He was blessed with many possessions, family, and wealth. But suddenly it is all stripped away from him. He loses everything. His family, gone. His possessions, gone. His physical health, gone. Job is grieving life as he once knew it. To top it all off, his friends come to console him but after several days, they began to berate him and accuse him of hiding some secret sin, idolizing things other than God, and more.

For chapters, Job and his friends go back and forth arguing about why Job is suffering. This is just adding more salt to Job's wounds. Eventually God speaks. God corrects Job's friends and also corrects Job for questioning Him. I love what Job says in his response to God, " *My ears had heard of you, but now my eyes have seen you*" (Job 42:5).

Job walked away from his suffering with a greater understanding and view of God. Not only this but God restored his fortunes and *"gave him twice as much as he had before"* (vs. 10).

While this is just a brief summary, the book of Job paints a beautiful picture of endurance. Suffering is hard to understand however we can rest assured that it is not in vain. Job thought his life was over, yet after he endured God restored him.

1 Peter 5:10 says, *"And the God of all grace, who called you to his eternal glory in Christ, after you have suffered a little*

while, will himself restore you and make you strong, firm, and steadfast."

The book of Job teaches us that we can trust that God is near, He is sovereign, and He will restore. Seasons of suffering won't last forever.

In seasons of suffering in your life or your clients' lives, remember that there is indeed a reward on the other side. Keep believing fellow helper.

Song for further encouragement:

Press - Maranda Curtis

| 94 |

Cheerleader

As helpers we can be some of our clients greatest cheerleaders, besides God of course. Have you ever sat across from a client and thought about how amazing of a person they are?

I can think of several clients who have entered my office wrestling with self-doubt, insecurity, and worthlessness.

They saw failure, brokenness, their mistakes, their flaws. They didn't believe that they were worthy of good things.

This breaks my heart but I can't say that I don't remember the days that I also believed some of these things about myself. There was a time when I could only see my faults, while everyone else saw all these things that I just could not see myself.

Eventually that changed by recognizing my inner critic, therapy, and an important prayer. I began to ask God to help me to see myself the way that He sees me." I prayed this prayer consistently for most of 2021 and God answered. He helped me to see myself as His daughter, as loved, as enough, as worthy, as accepted. He helped me to embrace the unique quirks, passions, and characteristics that He has birthed in me. And while the inner critic is still present, I am now able to confront it with truth and a renewed perspective of myself.

Today I find myself wanting my clients to be able to experience the same. Somedays I want to interrupt them and tell them just how amazing they are. I want them to know that they aren't a failure nor an embarrassment. However, I know that my words alone will not suffice. Their inner critic wouldn't let them believe it even if I tried.

As I work with clients who are seeking to challenge and transform the view of themselves, I now find myself asking God the same prayer on their behalf. I ask Him to help my clients to see themselves the way that He does. I encourage you to do the same fellow helper.

This prayer is such a powerful prayer because as we work with clients to recognize their inner critic and it's negative messages, it loses it's power. Truth can now become louder.

So whether your client needs it, or you need it, know that it is possible to quiet the badgering and nagging of our inner voice. It just takes time.

<u>Song for further reflection:</u>

You say - Lauren Daigle

| 95 |

Refreshed

To be refreshed is to be restored to a certain condition. The prefix re- means again. To be refreshed is to gain something again.

Many times I have had clients who leave my office and say something along the lines of "I needed this" or "I feel relieved." They are experiencing a refreshing.

The Bible tells us, *"The generous will prosper; those who refresh others will themselves be refreshed."* (Proverbs 11:25, NLT)

The moment I stumbled across this scripture God reminded me that as He works through me to provide spaces of refreshing for my clients, He is also my refresher.

Day after day you create a space for your clients to feel refreshed, fellow helper. As you give and pour, don't forget that God Himself will also refresh you. His Word guarantees that.

Look for His refreshing in a cold drink of water.
Look for His refreshing in the cool breeze as you walk outside.
Look for His refreshing on the sunny days where the sun hits your skin.
Look for His refreshing in quiet moments between sessions.
Look for His refreshing in silence.
Look for His refreshing in moments of rest.

Jeremiah 31:25 says, *"For I will satisfy the weary soul, and every languishing soul I will replenish"* (ESV). Believe that as you seek God, He won't fail to provide you with the refreshing that you are needing and longing for.

Prayer:

God I want to experience a refreshing. I want to be replenished. Replenished with energy, with motivation, with excitement, with hope. Lord I open my hands and I surrender my plans. I want to receive the refreshing you have for me. It's in your name I pray. Amen.

Truth for today:

God refreshes me so that I may do this work.

96

Can I do this?

Some days, I don't think I can do this. Some days I wonder if I am "cut out" for this work of counseling. What about you? Day in and day out, sitting with people who are seeking help for real life concerns? *Who am I to help them?*

This is an all too familiar voice. It's the voice of imposter syndrome. It's the part of me that doubts my abilities. That wonders if I am enough.

The term "imposter syndrome" was first coined in 1978 as "the imposter phenomenon" by psychologists Pauline Rose Clance, PhD, and Suzanne Imes, PhD. It's that little inner voice that causes us to question ourselves. Many of us are familiar with this voice.

This voice can interfere with our clinical work. It can cause us to overwork trying to compensate for our perceived lack of knowledge, or in other cases, shy away from opportunities. No matter how many accomplishments, positive client feedback, or years of learning, the imposter can weave it's way into our thoughts. It might even cause you an undue amount of anxiety as you prepare to sit with your clients.

Does this resonate? In moments that you begin to feel imposter syndrome seeping in, I encourage you to close your eyes and take some deep breaths. Focus your thoughts on the breaths you take and imagine pushing the voice of doubt away. It can be helpful to reflect on positive experiences. Maybe consider exceptions to the feeling, such as a moment that you have positively impacted a clients life. Maybe you have little experience with clients right now, perhaps it would be helpful to speak with a trusted mentor or supervisor about their experiences.

The main thing is this: You aren't alone fellow helper. Imposter syndrome is all too real and it's important that we talk about it and challenge it. Because you CAN do this. Today I pray that you would come to know and see that truth.

<u>Reflect:</u>

How has imposter syndrome shown up in my life?
Is it currently interfering with my ability to counsel those in my care?

<u>Read:</u>

Mark 9:23-24

97

Barriers

One of my favorite questions to get a client thinking about is, what are the barriers keeping them from achieving their wants, goals, and/or plans?

We all experience barriers and obstacles in our lives that may prevent us from getting to where we desire to go. For the person trying to eat healthier, a barrier might be their late night snacking. For the person who wants to wake up earlier to workout, a barrier might be snoozing alarms. For the person wanting a healthy romantic relationship, a barrier might be choosing unemotionally available partners.

Many clients come in wanting to change. They are wanting something in their life to be different however many times they haven't considered what patterns, things, or behaviors interfere with what they are wanting to accomplish. The same is true for ourselves.

As I think about this I am reminded of Hebrews 12:1-2 which says, *"...let us throw off everything that hinders and the sin that so easily entangles. And let us run with perseverance the race marked out for us, fixing our eyes on Jesus, the pioneer and perfecter of faith."*

Neither us nor our clients will be able to run this race of life, if we don't take time to consider what we need to throw off, what's hindering us, or what's entangling us. The therapeutic space is a great place to explore those barriers.

Some things may be preventing us from making the changes we desire and if we never pause to consider what those things might be, we may find ourselves stuck in the same patterns and ways.

<u>Reflect:</u>

Are there current barriers interfering with my current professional or personal goals?

| **98** |

Breathe

Hey fellow helper! Will you take a nice long deep breath with me? *Inhale-2-3-4, Hold-2-3-4, Exhale.* How are you doing today? How does your body feel? Are your shoulders relaxed or raised? How's your mind?

In the midst of busy schedules, endless to-do lists, and thoughts about all the things we need to do in a day, it can become easy to forget about the tension that can build up in our body. We begin to function on auto-pilot.

On several occasions I have locked myself out of the house. Rushing to work, thinking about too many things at once, carrying too many items, questioning if I forgot to blow out my candles or turn off the stove. Eventually I recognized that I was mentally exhausted, tense, and forgetful.

We can all fall into this pattern, it's not difficult to do at all. But we can correct it by listening to our body. By taking time to rest. By taking time to do nothing. By putting away the to-do list for a day. By taking time to breathe.

For 6 days God worked. He created the skies, the water, the land, the animals, the stars, and so much more. Genesis 2:2 says, *"On the seventh day God had finished his work of creation, so he rested from all his work."* In other words, God took a break. So we should too!

I imagine that you may have encouraged a client to take a break. You may have explored how they incorporate self-care and rest into their routine. You may have highlighted that their schedule is wearing them out. So let's not forget to consider our own need for self-care and rest.

As you go about your week, I pray that God would allow sweet opportunities of rest for you fellow helper. I pray for a cancellation when needed. I pray for someone to offer to watch your kids. I pray for someone to pay for a spa day. I pray for a chance to breathe. I pray that you would find space and opportunities to rest. Moments to breathe.

Take another deep breath with me. *Inhale-2-3-4, Hold-2-3-4, Exhale.* Have a great day fellow helper!

"Make it make sense"

Imagine being promised healing, recovery, or relief from God. You are struggling with some sickness, sin, or a heavy season. You begin to anticipate change. You begin to experience excitement for what's to come, only to see things start to get worse. Conditions get worse, things get harder...nothing is improving. You become discouraged. *Did I hear God right? Why did he tell me this?* What you see and what you were told isn't adding up. It doesn't make sense. You are told again, that it will happen. But at this point you just don't believe. *Make it make sense..*

This was the Israelites story. Stuck in harsh conditions in Egypt, the Israelites were promised that they would be led out of Egypt and into a land *"flowing with milk and honey"* (Exodus 3:8). Only, things begin to get worse for them in Exodus 5. So God promises again, *"'I am the Lord, and I will bring you out from under the yoke of the Egyptians. I will free you from being slaves to them"* (Exodus 6:6). However this time when Moses went to them, *"they did not listen to him because of their discouragement and harsh labor"* (Exodus 6:9). What the Israelites heard and what they saw didn't align, so they didn't believe. Sometimes we can have a hard time believing what we can't see, no matter how many times we are told.

The Israelites' story reminds us that God's promises require faith. Hebrews 11:1 says, *"Now faith is confidence in what we hope for and assurance about what we do not see."*

The Israelites did leave Egypt. And they did possess the promised land. It didn't occur in the timing they might've preferred and it surely wasn't how they expected, but it happened. They didn't expect things to get worse before they got better, but Pharaoh did eventually let them go.

<u>Reflect:</u>

What are you hoping for that you can't currently see? What have you been promised that you haven't seen come to pass?

As you consider the Israelites' story, I pray that you would experience an increase your faith fellow helper. I pray that when it doesn't make sense and things don't add up, you would once again be able to believe.

| 100 |

Encouraged

It's amazing how God will turn things around when we ask sometimes. One morning, I laid in bed dreading the day. I was tired, unmotivated, and discouraged. I began to rationalize, *it won't matter if I don't go to work, I'm not making a difference.*

I didn't want to go to work that day. I didn't want to sit with my clients. I just wanted to be. Before leaving the house, I remember asking God to help me feel purpose. To show me how I make a difference. Sluggish and teary eyed, I left my house and drove to work.

Some days I struggle to believe I am making a difference. Some days I leave work and just feel like everyone was going downhill and I couldn't help. Then there are days where God sends me little reminders that I am making a difference. That my presence does matter. That He is using me.

We won't always get to see the change, the seeds planted, or the warmth and safety clients feel by sitting with us. We won't always get to see or hear how we made an impact in their lives. But if we ask God, He'll show us.

Two people took time that day to tell me just how much of a difference I make/have made. I woke up discouraged. I ended my day encouraged.

You don't see it now, but be encouraged. You are making a difference fellow helper.

Prayer

Lord thank you for my fellow helper. Lord I pray right now for the helper reading this who has worked their way through each devotion and read every thought. I don't know what season they may find themselves in but God I know that you will meet them where they are. Whether they are beginning their counseling career, considering it, several years in, considering a career change, questioning their work, feeling burnt out, experiencing compassion fatigue, or a season of uncertainty. Lord your Word tells us that every need you will supply. Help my fellow helper to hold onto this truth.

Father continue speak to them and through them. Lord bless their clients, bless their family, bless their coworkers, bless them. Lord I pray that as they remain in this field, they would hold onto to John 15:5 which says, "I am the vine; you are the branches. If you remain in me and I in you, you will bear much fruit; apart from me you can do nothing." More than anything we recognize that we cannot do this work of caring for others without you because You are the Wonderful Counselor.

I pray that my fellow helper would surrender any expectations, desires, fears, insecurities, and outcomes to you. I pray that their work would glorify you and you would shine through them Lord. I pray that as they accept this call daily, they would always look to you. That they would run to you and seek you again and again and again. Father, thank you that you equipped them for this. It's in your name I pray. Amen.